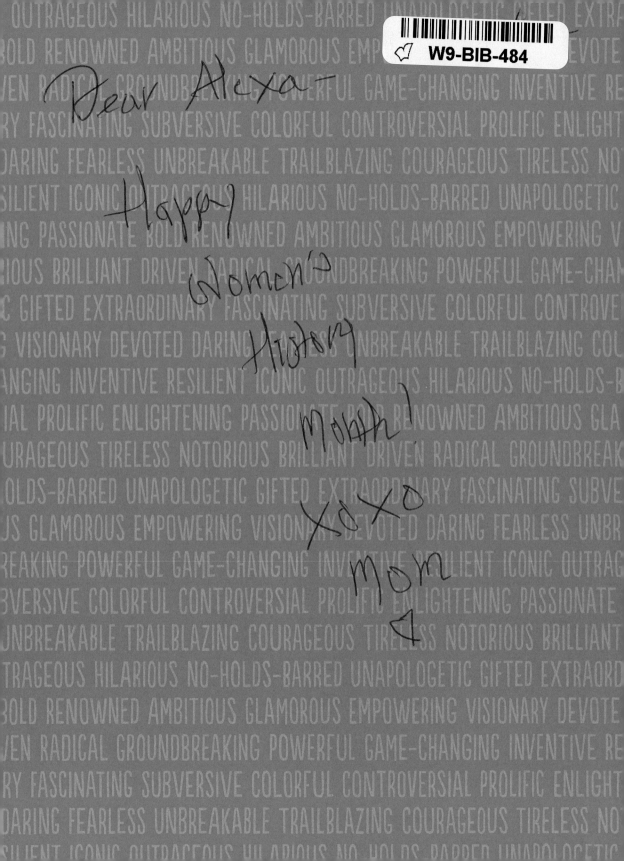

Dear Alexa—

Happy
Women's
History
Month!

XOXO

Mom
♡

AL GROUNDBREAKING POWERFUL GAME-CHANGING INVENTIVE RESILIENT IC
SUBVERSIVE COLORFUL CONTROVERSIAL PROLIFIC ENLIGHTENING PASSION
NBREAKABLE TRAILBLAZING COURAGEOUS TIRELESS NOTORIOUS BRILLIANT
TRAGEOUS HILARIOUS NO-HOLDS-BARRED UNAPOLOGETIC GIFTED EXTRAOR
BOLD RENOWNED AMBITIOUS GLAMOROUS EMPOWERING VISIONARY DEVO
DRIVEN RADICAL GROUNDBREAKING POWERFUL GAME-CHANGING INVENTIV
ARY FASCINATING SUBVERSIVE COLORFUL CONTROVERSIAL PROLIFIC ENLIG
DARING FEARLESS UNBREAKABLE TRAILBLAZING COURAGEOUS TIRELESS N
VE RESILIENT ICONIC OUTRAGEOUS HILARIOUS NO-HOLDS-BARRED UNAPOLO
IGHTENING PASSIONATE BOLD RENOWNED AMBITIOUS GLAMOROUS EMPOW
NOTORIOUS BRILLIANT DRIVEN RADICAL GROUNDBREAKING POWERFUL GAME
TIC GIFTED EXTRAORDINARY FASCINATING SUBVERSIVE COLORFUL CONTRO
ERING VISIONARY DEVOTED DARING FEARLESS UNBREAKABLE TRAILBLAZIN
L GAME-CHANGING INVENTIVE RESILIENT ICONIC OUTRAGEOUS HILARIOUS
ONTROVERSIAL PROLIFIC ENLIGHTENING PASSIONATE BOLD RENOWNED AM
ZING COURAGEOUS TIRELESS NOTORIOUS BRILLIANT DRIVEN RADICAL GROU
US NO-HOLDS-BARRED UNAPOLOGETIC GIFTED EXTRAORDINARY FASCINATIN
AMBITIOUS GLAMOROUS EMPOWERING VISIONARY DEVOTED DARING FEARL
GROUNDBREAKING POWERFUL GAME-CHANGING INVENTIVE RESILIENT ICONI
SUBVERSIVE COLORFUL CONTROVERSIAL PROLIFIC ENLIGHTENING PASSION
UNBREAKABLE TRAILBLAZING COURAGEOUS TIRELESS NOTORIOUS BRILLIANT
TRAGEOUS HILARIOUS NO-HOLDS-BARRED UNAPOLOGETIC GIFTED EXTRAOR
BOLD RENOWNED AMBITIOUS GLAMOROUS EMPOWERING VISIONARY DEVO
DRIVEN RADICAL GROUNDBREAKING POWERFUL GAME-CHANGING INVENT

"NICE" JEWISH GIRLS

BY JULIE MERBERG

ILLUSTRATIONS BY GEORGIA RUCKER

downtown bookworks

ACKNOWLEDGMENTS

I am beyond lucky to work with my psychic and gifted collaborator, Georgia Rucker, who magically makes every book look like something you'd want to read.

Thanks to Anna Collins for her sharp research and fact-checking.

I'm grateful to my "two Jews, three opinions" crew: Andrea Amiel, Marnie Berk, Julie Burden, Hannah Cramer, Natalie Cuchel, Janet Eisenberg, Gena Mann, Lulu Mann, Nancy Merberg, and Esther Perel for input, feedback, and cheerleading along the way.

My husband, David Bar Katz, constantly amazes me with his breadth of knowledge about Jewish history, and all the extremely helpful books he can pull off his shelves. And thank you to my temporarily neglected boys—Morris, Nathanael, Kal, and Maccabee—who kindly indulged my enthusiastic storytelling.

Immersing myself in so many incredible family histories was a stark reminder that my family would not be living the life we have if our brave and resilient Martz, Tinianow, Blinkoff, Merberg, Fleishman, Levin, and Katz ancestors had not taken on the enormous risks and challenges they did. Their journeys are the prologue to our story.

downtown bookworks

Downtown Bookworks Inc.
New York, New York
www.downtownbookworks.com
Copyright © 2021 Downtown Bookworks Inc.
Designed by Georgia Rucker
Printed in the United States of America, September 2021
10 9 8 7 6 5 4 3 2 1

DEDICATION

For my extraordinary tribe.

TABLE OF CONTENTS

If you spend enough time around Jewish women, you can't help but pick up on some common traits. On a personal level, there is warmth and humor with a dash of neurosis. We aggressively value education and social justice, family and community. I've always found an immediate level of comfort and familiarity when I meet other Jewish women, and that feeling spilled over into the women I profiled for this book. Reading their memoirs and biographies, watching and listening to interviews, documentaries, speeches, and performances, I *felt* like I knew them as I dug into their lives and unpacked their stories. I knew their noisy family dinners, their fierce drive, their uncanny ability to get stuff done.

The book is organized into themes, and at first I was surprised by how many wildly successful Jewish women thrived in similar fields. When I started my research and writing, three out of nine Supreme Court justices were Jewish—33 percent of the bench represented by a people who account for less than 3 percent of the population! I've experienced firsthand the importance Jewish women place on *tikkun olam*, or repairing the world. But the number and impact of Jewish activists would convince anyone that social justice is coded into our DNA.

The fact that each woman achieved what she did is astonishing, given the obstacles that are simply part of ordinary life. That many rose to prominence against a tide of anti-Semitism *and* sexism elevates their accomplishments, in some cases, from improbable to miraculous. The profiles are arranged chronologically within each section, an organization that highlights the evolving attitudes towards Jews and women over time. The historical women in the book were born in the late 1800s, shaped by the pogroms in Russia and eastern Europe, which drove them from their homes and destroyed any sense of security. For others, their lives were molded by the Holocaust. More contemporary subjects embrace their Judaism with an in-your-face pride that wasn't possible when we, as a people, were fighting for our lives.

As Jewish women have done for centuries, I've tried to create a community in the pages of this book. There are obviously many extraordinary women whom I didn't have the space to include. I wanted to focus on women whose contributions were significant and interesting, and whose connection to Judaism was meaningful, palpable, or relevant. The final list is not definitive or comprehensive—it's just where I landed. Their stories carry inspiration and lessons and unmistakable evidence of connection—cultural, spiritual, genetic, and otherwise—to you and to me. I hope you enjoy getting to know them as much as I have.

Julie Merberg

WARNING: *Jewish history sadly includes violence, oppression, persecution, and anti-Semitism. None of that has been scrubbed from these stories.*

ACTIVISTS

HENRIETTA SZOLD
1860–1945

Henrietta Szold didn't invent Zionism, but she turned the idea of it into a reality.

Born in Baltimore, Maryland, she was the first child of Rabbi Benjamin Szold and his wife Sophie. The Szolds had immigrated to the United States from Hungary a year before Henrietta's birth so that he could lead a Baltimore congregation. At the time, there were about 8,000 Jews living in the city. The rabbi was a modern thinker and taught Henrietta German, Hebrew, and sacred Jewish texts to supplement what she learned in public school. He also took her with him to the docks in Baltimore, where they would greet Jewish immigrants arriving from eastern Europe.

She was a gifted student and taught Hebrew school as a teenager and then became a full-time teacher as soon as she finished high school. She also began to write articles about Jewish culture in a number of national Jewish publications, making a name for herself as a writer.

Due to the reputation she'd established, in 1888 she became the only woman to work at the newly formed Jewish Publication Society which was founded to publish important Jewish works—from the Bible and prayer books to history and legends. Sophie worked there for 20 years, editing, translating, and publishing books. At night, she taught English to Russian Jewish immigrants and helped them settle into life in America with job training as well.

These roles put her in the center of Jewish intellectual life in America. It was the Russian intellectuals who got her thinking about establishing a Jewish community in Palestine. As a scholar and an intellectual, Henrietta was one of the first people to start talking about Zionism. In 1896, she gave a speech outlining her views: Jews should be allowed to return to their ancient homeland (in Palestine), and Jews—now spread out all over the world—should revive their traditional culture.

In 1902, Henrietta's father died. She moved to New York City and enrolled in the Jewish Theological Seminary (JTS) so that she could edit, translate, and publish her father's papers. The school was meant to train men to become rabbis, so she had to sign a letter promising that she would not become a rabbi in order to be allowed into classes. At JTS, she met other like-minded Zionists and joined study groups where they discussed the possibility of creating a Jewish homeland.

In 1909, Henrietta had had her fill of conversations about Zionism. Along with her 70-year-old mother, she set out to see Palestine for herself. They started their journey in Europe, visiting extended family in Hungary and working their way east through Alexandria, Beirut, and Damascus on the way to the Holy Land. The women rode around in a horse-drawn cart visiting farms in the Galilee. They walked through the narrow, winding streets of Jerusalem and were struck by the poverty and the terrible conditions that the Jews, Christians, and Muslims lived in there. They saw people blind from trachoma, a bacterial infection, due to lack of proper healthcare. It was clear to Henrietta and her

mother that there was lots of work to be done if this was to become a Jewish homeland. In spite of the very humble impressions, something about the place touched Henrietta's soul. As she described it in a letter to her friend, Judge Sulzberger, "It is not only the moon, the sky, the mountains, the caves, the air that are beautiful with an indescribable beauty.... It is a sentiment, as indescribable as the physical beauty."

After her six-month journey, Henrietta returned to New York quite changed. She was determined to put her brains, passion, and organizational skills to use doing what Jewish women have long excelled at: getting stuff done. She began by talking to women's groups about Palestine, explaining that the pioneers there sorely needed better hygiene and medical services. On Purim, in February 1912, she organized the first meeting of what would become Hadassah—a group of 38 women she had recruited from her study

ZIONISM

Zionism is a movement to return Jews to our ancient homeland in what was then Palestine and is now Israel. (In the Hebrew bible, the word *zion* refers to Israel and the city of Jerusalem.) The idea began to form in the 1880s as Jews were facing anti-Semitism and persecution around the world. Theodore Herzl, an Austrian Jewish journalist, is credited with establishing modern Zionism as a political organization in 1897. Herzl feared that Jews would not survive as a people without a homeland.

In 1923, the League of Nations (an early version of the United Nations that was created after World War I) gave Great Britain the job of establishing a Jewish homeland in Palestine. At the time, Palestine was under British control following the conclusion of the First World War. Between 1882 and 1914, about 75,000 European Jews made their way to Palestine, fleeing pogroms (waves of violence against Jews) and anti-Semitism. On May 14, 1948, the British army withdrew and Israel was declared an independent state. The next year, 249,000 settlers moved to Israel.

In 1950, Israel issued the Law of Return, which gives Jews born anywhere in the world the right to become an Israeli citizen.

groups got together at Temple Emanu-El on New York City's Upper East Side. Their goal was to create a large organization of women Zionists who would promote Jewish institutions and ventures in Palestine. Henrietta was elected president of the group.

She quickly started raising money to bring nurses to Palestine, realizing that good medical services were the most important first steps. In January 1913, she set sail with two nurses and the philanthropist Strauss family, who donated the funds to establish a nursing center. Two months later, they opened the American Daughters of Zion Nurses Settlement, Hadassah, in a rented house in Jerusalem. In the first year, they treated 5,000 patients.

In the meantime, new chapters of Hadassah were started in Jewish communities in other US cities, with the more ambitious goal of establishing a fully functioning hospital in Palestine. World War I slowed them down, but in 1918, they opened the American Zionist Medical unit with 45 doctors and nurses and modern medical equipment and technology. In 1920, Henrietta took over, transforming the hospital into the Hadassah Medical Organization.

Under her leadership, the hospital did much more to transform the lives of settlers. She established food programs, so that nobody would go hungry, and nurse training. All of this was financed by American Jews, and the hospital, by design, served people of every religious background. This monumental accomplishment was only the first in Henrietta Szold's transformation of the Zionist dream into a reality.

For the last 25 year of her life, she lived mostly in Palestine, traveling back to the States to see her sisters and meet with donors. She wanted to provide medical and educational services throughout Palestine. And she was determined to offer these services to Jews as well as to Arab citizens. This was a

"It seems to me I have not lived one life, but several, each one bearing its own character and insignia."

pretty radical position at the time, but she believed in what was then called a binational state. She held out hope that Jews and Arabs could live together peacefully.

In 1930, at the age of 70, the woman who had already moved mountains for 50 years took on the most important challenge of her life. Anti-Semitism was rampant in Europe by this point. In her own travels, Henrietta had seen signs at restaurants and inns warning "No Jews, No Dogs." And Jews were realizing the value in a safe haven, a Jewish homeland. German activists approached Henrietta for help in getting young people out of Germany and settled in Palestine. This involved working with the British government (which controlled Palestine) to secure visas. She needed funding for the ships that would transport the children. And, of course, the children would need support once they landed. They would have to be fostered or reconnected with relatives. They would need to be educated and learn a new language, and eventually they would need work. All of Henrietta's prior experiences—fundraising, creating services, settling refugees—and her endless compassion made her the perfect person to undertake this enormous challenge. In 1933, Henrietta took charge of an organization called Youth Aliyah, which helped bring 14,000 Jewish children from Germany to Palestine before and after World War II. It is astonishing to think about the number of lives Henrietta saved. What's more, she met every single boat that landed and made sure every single child was settled. And for the rest of her life, she made sure these children were educated and cared for.

She ran Youth Aliyah well into her 80s, until the day she died in the hospital she had built.

One of the children she rescued recited the Mourner's Kaddish at her funeral. Though it deeply saddened her that she never had children of her own, Henrietta Szold was very much the mother of Israel.

EMMA GOLDMAN

1869–1940

The typical Jewish woman born in Russia in 1869 was expected to marry young and raise a family, and not much else. According to Emma Goldman's father, "All a Jewish daughter needs to know is how to prepare gefilte fish, cut noodles fine, and give the man plenty of children," she recalled in her autobiography, *Living My Life*.

Born in the Jewish quarter of Kovno, a city in what was then part of the Russian Empire, Emma's family moved from one Jewish ghetto (a part of the city where only Jews lived) to another, attempting to escape anti-Semitism. Their last stop was in St. Petersburg, a Russian city that was considered more tolerant than most of Russia because it allowed certain skilled, privileged Jews to live and work there.

When Emma was 16, she had had enough of Russia's unfair treatment of Jews and her father's strict rules. She convinced her parents, Abraham and Taube, to let her emigrate to the United States with her older, beloved sister, Helena. She recalled, "I left without regrets. Since my earliest recollection, home had been stifling, my father's presence terrifying. My mother, while less violent with the children, never showed much warmth. It was always Helena who gave me affection, who filled my childhood with whatever joy it had."

The two sisters savored their first taste of freedom when they spotted the Statue of Liberty as they headed into New York Harbor. They made their way to Rochester, New York, where another sister, Lena, had already settled with her husband—along with a community of Russian Jews.

Emma easily found work in a glove factory earning $2.50 a week, which, it turned out, was just barely enough to cover her room, board, and travel expenses. So she boldly decided to explain the situation to her boss and ask him for a raise. He refused on the grounds that he would then have to give all of the other factory workers a raise as well. This was Emma's first direct exposure to the exploitation of immigrant labor. As her boss knew, most people making so little money would put up with a measly salary because it was better than no income at all. Emma soon quit when she found a new job in a smaller clothing workshop closer to home making $4 a week.

She married a fellow worker and settled into a traditional life her father would have approved of, consoling herself that at least she'd chosen her husband and had a decent job. But that arrangement got old fast. She still wasn't earning much money, and the work was boring. Her husband wasn't adventurous. On top of feeling stifled, she experienced what she later described as her spiritual birth.

On May 1, 1886, more than 300,000 workers throughout the country went on strike demanding an 8-hour workday. Up to that point, 12-hour workdays were common. Three days after the May Day strike, there was another peaceful protest—this time against police shootings of striking workers in Chicago. During this protest, a bomb was set off in an area of Chicago called Haymarket Square. Anarchist organizers of the strike were blamed for the bombing and later found guilty in an unfair trial. Seven of the eight accused were sentenced to death. Emma and Helena were closely following this story and the fate of the anarchists in the newspapers. The death sentence was Emma's call to action. She identified with the laborers and wanted to fight for their cause on behalf of the men who were unjustly punished.

And just like that, in 1889, Emma left Rochester and her husband and fled to New York City with $5 and a sewing machine. She found her way to the address of an acquaintance she had met at a labor meeting in Rochester, and he introduced her to the Yiddish Lower East Side. This neighborhood in lower Manhattan was teeming with Jewish immigrants speaking German, Russian, and Yiddish. They worked all day in the city's sweatshops and factories and came home

WHAT IS AN ANARCHIST?

An anarchist is someone who rebels against any kind of authority or ruling power. Anarchists believe in absolute freedom—and that given free choice, people are good and will create just systems. Some anarchists believed in peaceful protests, while others felt that violence was necessary to achieve change.

to crowded tenements. At night, men and women climbed to the roofs for fresh air and met in cafes and bars where anarchists worked, planned, and debated.

Emma quickly befriended the leaders of the anarchist movement, including Alexander (Sasha) Berkman, who became her boyfriend, and Johann Most, editor of *Freiheit*, an anarchist newspaper. Shortly after they met, Emma went to Central Park with Most for a picnic, and he talked about "his hatred of the capitalist system, his vision of a new society of beauty and joy for all." As they walked and talked, Emma noticed the mansions lining the park and observed that it was unfair that so few people held so much wealth, while others lived in poverty in tiny, cramped apartments on the Lower East Side. Most, who was already a famous, sought-after lecturer, identified the same charisma and public-speaking skills in Emma and decided to mentor her.

Speaking in German and Yiddish, she began to lecture other immigrants in New York City who were also eager to improve their working conditions and hours. As soon as she had refined her speeches and delivery, she started touring the country to spread the anarchists' message. She met with laborers—steelworkers, garment and textile workers, woodworkers, farmers, and others—encouraging them to organize and fight for shorter hours, better pay, and the creation of unions.

As someone who understood Torah study and the value of questioning and challenging ideas, Emma's background prepared her for life as a social justice crusader. At the same time, she rejected organized religion, including Judaism. An atheist, she made a point of protesting on Yom Kippur. Emma was not one to follow anybody's rules. Even in a community of radicals, Emma stood out as extreme. At a time when Jewish girls married in their teens and early 20s, she believed in "free love." She explained, "If I ever love a man again, I will give myself to him without being bound by the rabbi or the law, and when that love dies, I will leave without permission." Anti-marriage, she argued for gay rights in the 1890s, a full century ahead of her time. Though she believed in women's equality, she did not support the women's suffrage movement because she thought that politics were corrupt, and voting wouldn't fix that. Perhaps most radical of all, in 1892, when she and Sasha Berkman read that Henry Clay Frick, who ran the Carnegie Steel Company mills, had fired striking unionized workers asking for more pay, they quickly decided that Frick must be assassinated. Sasha's unsuccessful attempt to do just that landed him in prison for 14 years.

> "I want freedom, the right to self-expression, everybody's right to beautiful, radiant things."

Though police were unable to connect Emma to the assassination plot, she, too, wound up in jail within the year for inciting a riot while rallying a crowd of thousands of unemployed laborers in New York City's Union Square. "If they do not give you work, demand bread. If they deny you both, take bread," she urged. Ten months in a cold, dank prison left her more determined than ever to continue her fight. The government "can never stop women from talking," she insisted.

Emma became a famous speaker, lecturing around the country on the importance of freedom—whether it was freedom from government oppression or free speech or a woman's right to birth control. One of the many things she was arrested for was distributing birth control pamphlets, which was illegal. She was arrested so often that she took to carrying a book around with her so that she would have something to read in jail.

In 1916, as the United States seemed likely to join the fighting in World War I, Emma threw her energy into opposing the war. She felt that wars were fought by the working class to protect and benefit the wealthy and urged men to protest the draft. This led to her arrest in 1917 and a two-year prison sentence, after which she was deported to the Soviet Union. She continued to rail against authority wherever she lived and traveled, finally moving to Canada, where she lived out her days helping refugees and immigrants, putting up a fight any time she sensed a whiff of oppression.

BETTY FRIEDAN
1921–2006

> "The problem lay buried, unspoken, for many years in the minds of American women. It was a strange stirring, a sense of dissatisfaction, a yearning that women suffered in the middle of the twentieth century in the United States. . . ."
>
> —from *The Feminine Mystique*

The Feminine Mystique, Betty Friedan's groundbreaking book published in 1963, pulled back the curtain on a feeling of emptiness she had been experiencing. As described on the very first page, she discovered that other suburban housewives were feeling the same way: "As she made the beds, shopped for groceries, matched slipcover material, ate peanut butter sandwiches with her children, chauffeured Boy Scouts and Brownies, lay beside her husband at night—she was afraid to ask herself the silent question—'Is this all?'" Millions of women read the book and identified with its premise—that shaping an identity solely as a mother and wife, without a career or creative outlet or a chance to find fulfillment and success independently, just wasn't enough.

Betty began researching and writing her book in 1957, initially through a questionnaire sent to 200 women who had graduated with her from Smith College. At this time, women were starting to marry younger (often in their teens!), and fewer were attending college. Among those who did go to college, more were getting married and having babies while they were still in school. Fewer and fewer women were working. While some were content with their homemaking role, many felt trapped. Then along came Betty Friedan, challenging the myth of "the feminine mystique" and, in part, triggering what would become the women's liberation movement.

She was particularly concerned about the harmful, negative stereotypes depicting Jewish mothers as controlling and manipulative. Betty grew up in Peoria, Illinois, where her father, Harry Goldstein, an immigrant from Kiev, Ukraine, became a successful jeweler. Her mother, Miriam, was the women's page editor of the Peoria newspaper—a job she loved—until she gave it up to raise her children. The family was barred from the Peoria country club, where all of their gentile friends belonged. (Many private clubs did not accept Jews at the time.) Socially isolated, Miriam blamed her immigrant husband—his accent and his differentness—rather than the community itself for their anti-Semitism. As Betty grew to understand, Miriam also harbored a lot of anger over the fact that she had given up her career, anger that she directed at Harry.

As a teenager, Betty experienced the sting of anti-Semitism as well. When she got to high school, she was dropped by all of her friends and rejected by high school sororities (which were a thing at that time). While anti-Semitism drove Miriam to distance herself from her Judaism, it eventually drove Betty to embrace it. "Ever since I was a little girl, I remember my father telling me that I had a passion for justice. But I think it was really a passion against injustice which originated from my feelings of the injustice of anti-Semitism," she explained.

At Smith College, a prestigious women's college in Northampton, Massachusetts, Betty was shocked to discover more self-hatred among her Jewish classmates. On November 9, 1938, when she was a freshman, Nazis in Germany burned synagogues and destroyed Jewish homes and businesses, killing 100 Jews and later arresting 30,000 more in an outpouring of violence and hatred known as Kristallnacht (which translates to "Night of Broken Glass"). In response, the college president William Neilson created a petition, which he urged students to sign, asking President Roosevelt to let German Jewish girls enter the US, outside of the current immigration quotas, in order to enroll at Smith. This was an effort to save German Jews from what would clearly be a terrible fate. Each student house discussed the proposal, and Betty's four Jewish housemates argued against it and refused to sign! They did not want to be known as Jews. Though Betty spoke out in favor of welcoming girls fleeing persecution, the petition was rejected by the majority of students.

After she graduated, Betty went on to study psychology but felt that her advanced education was intimidating to men. She then worked as a journalist, married Carl Freidan, and was eventually fired for being pregnant. A full-time mother of three when she researched

SECOND WAVE FEMINISM

The feminist movement called the "second wave" kicked off in the 1960s. Whereas the first wave of feminism in the early 1900s focused on women's suffrage, (the right to vote), the second wave pushed for equal rights for women. Women organized and lobbied for equal pay, an end to job discrimination, reproductive rights, and other legal protections for women. Betty Friedan, Gloria Steinem (page 24), and Bella Abzug (page 136) were three of the most prominent leaders of this movement.

ERA YES

and wrote *The Feminine Mystique*, she grew to realize that she had been repressed both as a woman and as a Jew. She reclaimed her Jewish identity as she found her feminist voice.

While the book made her famous, Betty did not stop at calling attention to the problem. She then helped galvanize women to fix it. In 1966, she cofounded the National Organization for Women (NOW), a civil rights group dedicated to achieving equality of opportunity for women. In 1969, she helped found the National Association for the Repeal of Abortion Laws (which is now known as NARAL Pro-Choice America). In 1970, on the 50th anniversary of the passage and ratification of the 19th Amendment, which gave women the right to vote, Betty organized the Women's Strike for Equality. Fifty thousand women marching down Fifth Avenue in New York City proved that feminism was not some fringe movement—and it wasn't going away. In 1971, she and other feminist leaders established the National Women's Political Caucus.

Opinionated, abrasive, and forceful even in a community of strong feminists, Betty didn't get along with everyone. She lagged in supporting gay rights (she did not want that issue to define the movement). And her work didn't acknowledge the additional challenges faced by women of color or those who *had* to work menial jobs to make a living. But she spent most of her life teaching, marching, and speaking out on behalf of women's equality in the US—continuing the conversation she had started. And her focus on Jewish women in particular was ongoing.

Widely considered to be the mother of second-wave feminism, Betty characterized herself as a Jewish feminist.

JEWISH WOMEN IN THE HOMELAND

In 1984, Betty led the American delegation to a conference of the American Jewish Congress in Israel. Entitled "Women as Jews, Jews as Women," the meeting led to the founding of the Israel Women's Network (IWN), which grew into a powerful political group demanding gender equality in Israel.

GLORIA STEINEM

1934–

According to traditional Jewish law, Gloria Steinem is not technically Jewish because her mother was gentile, a Presbyterian—only her father was Jewish. But Gloria has explained, "Wherever there is anti-Semitism, I identify as a Jew." An activist who has always relished her role as an outsider, she is also regarded as a Jew by the outside world, for better or worse. During the heyday of the women's rights movement in the 1970s, far right extremists considered feminism a Jewish conspiracy to kill Christian babies, since Gloria, along with Betty Friedan (page 20), Bella Abzug (page 136), and many other Jewish feminists sought to legalize abortion.

Gloria was not the first activist in the family. Her paternal grandmother, Pauline Steinem, was a well-known suffragist. In the mid-1930s, Pauline, whose father was a cantor, also helped members of her family escape from Germany. At that time, before World War II, it was possible to get a Jew out of Germany and into Palestine. Pauline, who had emigrated to the United States from Germany when she was 19, could see where things were heading for German Jews and paid to bring as many family members as she could to safety. Gloria was only five years old when her grandmother died and didn't know her very well. Gloria later recalled, "They told me that she was a wonderful woman who kept a kosher table, had four sons, and was a pioneer of vocational education . . . but not that she was also the first woman to be elected to a Board of Education in the state of Ohio. . . . In a way, feminism rediscovered my grandmother for me."

Gloria's mother, Ruth, wielded a different type of influence on her life. Much like Gloria, Ruth dreamed of being a writer at a time when women had to write under a man's name. "My mother was a pioneer in journalism before I was born, but she couldn't make it all work together to be the perfect wife and mother and to have a pioneering career at the same time." Ruth gave up her career in order to raise Gloria and her older sister, Susanne. Ruth then suffered from depression to the point where Gloria became her mother's caretaker. And that childhood experience led Gloria to make the opposite choice: to avoid marriage and family so that she could have a meaningful career. From the moment she left home—first to spend her senior year of high school with her sister in Washington, D.C., and then to go to the all-female Smith College, Gloria's family, community, and cohorts have always been circles of strong women.

She went to college in an era when "women were being educated to be mothers and the wives of executives." When she graduated and embarked on a career as a freelance writer, Gloria became frustrated with her inability to publish articles about the issues that interested her—women's issues such as workplace equality, domestic violence,

> "A lot of my generation are living out the un-lived lives of our mothers."

and reproductive rights. It was a very different time. "There was no word for sexual harassment. It was just called life. So you had to find your individual way around it."

In addition to writing, Gloria volunteered for Cesar Chavez's United Farm Workers union and for Robert F. Kennedy's political campaign, where she got frontline organizing and political training. When she was covering an abortion rights speak-out in Greenwich Village in 1968, she had a revelation. Gloria had an illegal abortion in 1957, and as she listened to women share their painful stories of illegal abortions, it struck her: "If one in three women has needed an abortion in her lifetime in this country, then why is it a secret and why is it criminal and why is it dangerous?" Her life took on new meaning and a new cause: she was a feminist.

Because Gloria was such an effective, charismatic, mediagenic communicator, she quickly became the face of and spokesperson for the movement. She began to speak to groups of women at colleges and community centers with partner Dorothy Pitman Hughes, a Black activist. On the road, in these rooms full of receptive, enthusiastic, women who shared both her frustration with gender inequality and her desire for women's liberation, Gloria "began to understand that my experience was an almost universal female experience."

A BUNNY'S TALE

In 1963, Gloria first made a name for herself by writing an exposé about the degrading working conditions for the cocktail waitresses, known as Playboy bunnies, at a chain of restaurants called the Playboy Club. Waitresses had to wear revealing, cleavage-baring outfits with rabbit ears and cotton tails. Gloria went undercover for the assignment.

She cofounded *Ms.* magazine with Dorothy Pitman Hughes. It first appeared as an insert in *New York* magazine and then as a stand-alone publication, in July 1972. The name *Ms.* was an identifier that wasn't tied to a woman's marital status. The 300,000 test copies of that first magazine—intended to last for three months—sold out in just eight days.

Along with congresswomen Bella Abzug and Shirley Chisolm and other prominent activists, politicians, and civil rights leaders, she cofounded the National Women's Political Caucus in 1971. The organization's goal was to increase women's participation in political life. "I learned to use anger constructively," she has explained. That same very busy year, she also founded the Women's Action Alliance, the first national clearinghouse for information and technical assistance on women's issues and projects. Working with these groups, she helped to get the Equal Rights Amendment (ERA) passed by the House of Representatives in 1971 and by the Senate in 1972.

Gloria spent years inspiring women and patiently explaining the importance of equality—and the ways in which the world was not equal for women and men—to everyone else. Early on she knew "you have to uproot racism and sexism at the same time, otherwise it just doesn't work." Later in life, she connected racism and sexism to anti-Semitism as well, all means of oppression.

Having made an enormous impact on equal protections for American women over the last half century, Gloria continues to advocate for equal rights around the world. Though she shows no signs of slowing down, she offered these words of wisdom for the next generation of feminists: "Do not listen to my advice. Listen to the voice inside you and follow that."

ALICIA GARZA

1981–

Black, Jewish, queer, and born in Oakland, California, in the 1980s, Alicia Schwartz may have been destined to become an activist.

Her life as a Jew began when Alicia was four years old and her Black mother married her Jewish stepfather. Alicia took his name and embraced Judaism. The family moved from Oakland to the very white and more affluent neighborhood of Tiburon, north of San Francisco, where Alicia was acutely aware of being one of very few Black students during her school years. Though she felt like an outsider, "I grew up with the ethos that you always fight for the underdog," she has said.

Alicia's life in activism began at the age of 12, when she worked to promote sex education in her middle school. At the time, many schools were focusing on teaching abstinence rather than sharing information about birth control, and, like her mother, Alicia felt it was important for girls to have the facts. She continued to defend reproductive rights in high school.

As a college student at the University of California, San Diego, Alicia rallied to increase janitors' wages and helped to launch the campus's Women of Color Conference. She studied sociology and anthropology, and after she graduated, social justice quickly became her life's work.

In 2003, Alicia began an internship at School of Unity and Liberation (SOUL) in Oakland, California, a group that trained organizers. (There she met her future husband, Malachi Garza, a transgender community activist.) Next, she worked with People United for a Better Life in Oakland (PUEBLO), and then it was on to People Organized to Win Employment Rights (POWER). Throughout the decade, Alicia learned how to organize the hard way: by knocking on doors and having conversations with her neighbors throughout Oakland. The work was about uniting residents—to oppose a Walmart (they lost), to provide public funding for neighborhood improvements such as burying power lines underground, and to create and protect affordable housing. Over and over again, Alicia helped identify issues that unfairly hurt people of color or people who were poor—or both. Then she would devise effective means of attempting to right the wrong through organizing.

In 2012, everything changed. In Florida, a white Hispanic man named George Zimmerman shot and killed an unarmed Black teenager named Trayvon Martin during an argument on the street. Zimmerman pleaded self-defense and was found not guilty at his 2013 trial by a jury of five white women and one Latina.

Devastated by the verdict, Alicia wrote a powerful, passionate "love letter to Black folks" on Facebook that concluded with "I continue to be surprised at how little Black lives matter. Our lives matter."

BLACK LIVES
MATTER

Her friend and fellow activist Patrisse Cullors shared the post with the hashtag #BlackLivesMatter. A movement was born.

As the hashtag blew up on social media, the women, along with another friend, Opal Tometti, decided to formalize the movement with a website, a platform, and chapters all around the country. As Alicia explains in her book *The Purpose of Power*, "Hashtags do not start movements—people do." Over the next seven years, there were dozens of tragic murders of Black men and women, often at the hands of police: Eric Garner, Tamir Rice, Freddie Gray, Philando Castile, Ahmaud Arbery, and Breonna Taylor are just some of the higher profile cases that gave people a window into the kind of injustices that had been going on for many years before cell phones and body cameras exposed them. With Black Lives Matter, people channeled their grief and anger into the largest protest movement in history. By the summer of 2020, on the heels of George Floyd's murder, millions of people of every color, ethnicity, and age united to protest systemic racism in America. And Alicia's words, "Black Lives Matter," was their rallying cry.

"Movements are the story of how we come together when we've come apart."

In 2017, while the movement was still growing, Alicia stepped away from her leadership role and took what felt like the natural next step in her activism, founding Black Futures Lab. Her thinking was to go beyond protesting and to actually change the rules and impact laws to actively make Black lives matter. The group set about surveying Black voters and then shaping an agenda that included goals such as increasing the minimum wage and creating home ownership opportunities—things that would help people in their daily lives. During the pandemic, they drafted a "COVID-19 Relief and Recovery Plan for Black America." Many of the ideas that grew out of the Black Futures Lab found their way into the relief bills passed by Congress.

In other words, Alicia is already realizing her goal of "winning real things for real people." And she is far from finished.

HEDY LAMARR RESILIENT JOAN RIVERS ICONIC BARBRA STREISAND OUT
SILVERMAN HILARIOUS TIFFANY HADDISH UNAPOLOGETIC ABBI JACOBSON N
D ILANA GLAZER INVENTIVE HEDY LAMARR RESILIENT JOAN RIVERS ICONIC
SAND OUTRAGEOUS SARAH SILVERMAN HILARIOUS TIFFANY HADDISH UNAPO
JACOBSON NO-HOLDS-BARRED ILANA GLAZER INVENTIVE HEDY LAMARR RE
VERS ICONIC BARBRA STREISAND OUTRAGEOUS SARAH SILVERMAN HILARIOU
H UNAPOLOGETIC ABBI JACOBSON NO-HOLDS-BARRED ILANA GLAZER INVEN
RESILIENT JOAN RIVERS ICONIC BARBRA STREISAND OUTRAGEOUS SARAH
S TIFFANY HADDISH UNAPOLOGETIC ABBI JACOBSON NO-HOLDS-BARRED IL
TIVE HEDY LAMARR RESILIENT JOAN RIVERS ICONIC BARBRA STREISAND OUT
SILVERMAN HILARIOUS TIFFANY HADDISH UNAPOLOGETIC ABBI JACOBSON N
D ILANA GLAZER INVENTIVE HEDY LAMARR RESILIENT JOAN RIVERS ICONIC
SAND OUTRAGEOUS SARAH SILVERMAN HILARIOUS TIFFANY HADDISH UNAPO
JACOBSON NO-HOLDS-BARRED ILANA GLAZER INVENTIVE HEDY LAMARR RE
VERS ICONIC BARBRA STREISAND OUTRAGEOUS SARAH SILVERMAN HILARIOU
H UNAPOLOGETIC ABBI JACOBSON NO-HOLDS-BARRED ILANA GLAZER INVEN
RESILIENT JOAN RIVERS ICONIC BARBRA STREISAND OUTRAGEOUS SARAH
S TIFFANY HADDISH UNAPOLOGETIC ABBI JACOBSON NO-HOLDS-BARRED ILA
TIVE HEDY LAMARR RESILIENT JOAN RIVERS ICONIC BARBRA STREISAND OUT
SILVERMAN HILARIOUS TIFFANY HAD SON ICONIC

ENTERTAINERS

D ILANA GLAZER INVENTIVE HEDY L/
D OUTRAGEOUS SARAH SILVERMAN HILARIOUS TIFFANY HADDISH UNAPOLO
N NO-HOLDS-BARRED ILANA GLAZER INVENTIVE HEDY LAMARR RESILIENT
BARBRA STREISAND OUTRAGEOUS SARAH SILVERMAN HILARIOUS TIFFANY

HEDY LAMARR

1914–2000

Hedy Lamarr's story is grander and more glamorous than any of the characters she played on screen. Hedwig Eva Maria Kiesler was born in 1914 in Vienna, Austria, to assimilated Jewish parents. Her father was a banker, and her mother, a concert pianist. A striking beauty, Hedy was discovered while a teenager by Russian Jewish director Alexis Granowski. He exposed her to a circle of Russian Jewish artists whom she worked with, appearing at first in small roles in films throughout Europe. She became a sensation after starring in a racy Czech film called *Ecstasy* in 1933. In 1934, she married Fritz Mandl, a wealthy Austrian Jewish munitions manufacturer who sold weapons to the Nazis.

Her husband's attempts to control her (which included buying up all copies of *Ecstasy*) were just one of the reasons she ended the first of her six marriages. She fled their home on bicycle in the middle of the night, disguised as a maid—a maid bound for Hollywood. On the ship from London to New York, she met Metro Goldwyn Mayer (MGM) studio head Louis B. Mayer. Smitten, he gave her a contract with MGM, and she took the name Hedy Lamarr. She became an instant star upon the release of her first American film, *Algiers*, in 1938. And she continued to make popular movies for the next 20 years with screen legends, including Clark Gable and Spencer Tracy. The 1949 Cecil B. DeMille epic *Samson and Delilah* is one of her best known films. She was considered by many at the time to be the most beautiful woman in the world, her fair skin, green eyes, and delicate features inspiring the cartoon beauties Snow White and Catwoman. And during the peak of her popularity in the 1940s, plastic surgery patients requested this Jewess's profile more than anyone else's.

But Hedy wasn't about to get by on her looks and wasn't comfortable hanging out in Hollywood making lots of money when the world was in such a state. She was also a brilliant inventor who turned her talents to helping out with the war effort. In 1942, while other leading ladies were attending parties and premieres, she set out to create a device that would block enemy ships from jamming torpedo guidance signals. Perhaps remembering dinner party conversations with her ex-husband's military friends, she asked her friend and fellow inventor, composer George Antheil, to help her develop a concept that would become known as frequency hopping. Patented as the "secret communications system," it was based on the idea that the radio guidance transmitter and the torpedo's receiver would switch from frequency to frequency at the same time, making it impossible for the enemy to locate and block the message before it moved.

Although the concept could not be put to use during the war due to limited technology, years later it became the basis of spread-spectrum communications that secure military communications and

> "I'm an important star and lived a full life, yet I only have three close friends. I guess that's all anyone can expect."

cell phones. During the 1962 Cuban missile crisis, all of the US ships circling Cuba were armed with torpedoes guided by this frequency-hopping system. Hedy's concept of wireless communications using variable signals later became a key component in Bluetooth, WiFi, and GPS as well! Later in her life, when the importance of her invention was fully realized, she was honored with the 1997 Pioneer Award of the Electronic Frontier Foundation.

For much of her life, even as she helped raise millions of dollars in war bonds, Hedy denied her Jewish heritage. Louis B. Mayer had originally encouraged her to do so, worried that audiences would not fantasize about a Jew during a time of such intense anti-Semitism. In 1964, she went to see the film *The Pawnbroker*, a stark drama about a Holocaust survivor and ongoing anti-Semitism. She was so distraught by the film that she walked out, went into a department store, and wound up being arrested for shoplifting. Her relationship with Judaism was certainly complicated.

In spite of all of her accomplishments, "the most beautiful woman in the world" felt a lot of pressure to stay that way, leading her to undergo some unfortunate plastic surgery. She spent the latter part of her life as something of a recluse. She died in Casselberry, Florida, in January 2000, leaving behind three adult children and a fascinating legacy.

HIGH FLYING INVENTIONS

Hedy dated the notorious aviation entrepreneur Howard Hughes in the 1940s. She helped him develop a new wing shape for his planes to make them more aerodynamic. And he supplied her with a team of scientists to help her execute her ideas. Over the course of her life, she invented many things, including a fluorescent dog collar, modifications for the supersonic Concorde airliner, and a new kind of stoplight.

JOAN RIVERS
1933–2014

Joan was the second daughter of Beatrice and Meyer Molinsky, both Russian immigrants. Meyer was a doctor, and the family lived on "Doctors' Row" in the Brownsville section of Brooklyn. Though Meyer had grown up poor, his work provided a nice lifestyle for the family. Joan and her older sister went to Brooklyn Ethical Culture, a private school, when they were young. The family moved to a house in the suburb of Larchmont and belonged to a country club there. Still, these comforts were not enough for Beatrice, whose family had been wealthy before they had to leave it all behind in Russia. Joan remembers her mother always wanting more—more spending money, more extravagance. Joan also noted that without a job, her mother was completely dependent on her father's income.

A desire to be fully independent and a bit of an immigrant mentality—that everything could disappear overnight—may have driven Joan's relentless work ethic and quest for success after success in career after career.

Joan realized she wanted to spend her life onstage when she was six years old, donning cat ears for her very first stage role as a kitten in her school play. From that moment on, she was driven to be a star. But her path to stardom was far from quick and easy.

She spent her tween years feeling self-conscious and unattractive. A very bright student, she went to Barnard College in New York City. (Her older sister was the only girl at Columbia Law School.) Nice Jewish parents, the Molinskys were happy to support their daughters' educations. They were not so keen on Joan's acting ambitions. Though she appeared in some campus productions, after graduating Joan first attempted a more traditional career path as a buyer for a department store. This was followed by a brief marriage to the son of the store's owner.

When her marriage ended in 1958, Joan headed to a photo booth, took a bunch of pictures of herself making different expressions, and then used those photos as her headshot. Her show business career did not get off to a roaring start. Joan performed stand-up—not very well—in small comedy clubs and coffeehouses in New York City. She landed a few minor roles in a few tiny plays. One of those plays, *Driftwood*, also featured a then unknown teenage Barbra Streisand. (See page 39.) She was hired and fired from comedy writing jobs. Her career sputtered along and she remained determined to make it in what was then very much a man's world, trying to share the humor of her life as an insecure single woman. (Early on, she also dropped her extremely ethnic name, Molinsky, and became Joan Rivers.)

In the summer of 1965, she met producer Edgar Rosenberg and married him four days later. He would become her producer and business partner. That same year, Joan had her big break. *The Tonight Show with Johnny Carson* was the most popular show in America, and Joan was invited on as a guest. During her years performing stand-up comedy, she had developed a new style, inspired by Lenny Bruce and Elaine May, that was more storytelling than joke telling. Her own life became her comedy. Wearing a prim black cocktail dress and pearls, Joan regaled Johnny with hilarious, racy stories about newlywed life, cooking, and her husband. The audience, and Johnny, ate it up. With tears in his eyes from laughing, Johnny told Joan, "You're very funny. You're going to be a star." And he was right.

He also helped propel her to stardom over the next decade with regular appearances and a guest-hosting gig on *The Tonight Show*. These, in turn, led to more TV appearances and performances and her own daytime talk show, *That Show with Joan Rivers*. She released Grammy-nominated comedy albums (that was a thing) and a bestselling autobiography, *Enter Talking*. She had a daughter, Melissa. She was filling huge theaters around the country with adoring fans.

And she filled filing cabinets with jokes and routines, all organized by theme: pets, self-worth, children. By the 1980s, everybody knew who Joan Rivers was—the dirty, daring Jewish funny lady. And then she was offered the ultimate prize, her own late-night talk show with Fox.

She accepted the offer, and her mentor, Johnny Carson, stopped speaking to her. His network (NBC) also cut her off because she was now competing with them. Edgar produced *The Late Show Starring Joan Rivers*, which premiered in 1986. And then, at the height of her stardom, just as her immigrant mother had always feared, everything she had built disappeared almost overnight. The show was cancelled. Edgar committed suicide. And nobody would return her phone calls.

Devastated personally and professionally, after sitting shiva in her now lonely home in Belair, California, she moved to New York,

summoned her chutzpah, and started over. "I never thought anything was beneath me. I have to make a living . . . I'd do anything to stay in the business," she explained. Initially "anything" meant a game show called *Hollywood Squares*. Ultimately a daytime talk show, a successful radio show that was syndicated around the country. More bestselling books. A jewelry line that she sold on QVC—with sales ultimately totaling $1 billion!

Over and over, when people told her she was too Jewish, too raunchy, too inappropriate, she knew who she was. Her career was about proving everyone wrong. "Don't you dare tell me I can't do it" was her refrain. And then in her 70s, when most people would have kicked up their feet and retired in their extravagant townhouse, she launched her next career as a fashion commentator on the E! network with her daughter as cohost.

In *Joan Rivers: A Piece of Work*, a 2010 documentary about a year in her exceptionally busy life, the 70-something diva is seen hustling nonstop. She complains about the glare of an empty calendar, poring through page after page, year after year, where she is booked up nearly every minute of every day performing, traveling, selling, writing . . . always, always working. Her lavish, palatial home, gigantic jewels, designer clothes, and dedicated staff appear throughout the film. It is pretty clear that she doesn't *need* to work. Except that her work is who she is. She is still the awkward Jewish girl who made a career out of mocking herself, who transformed her insecurity and outsiderness into extraordinary success. She explains, "This is where I belong. The only time I'm truly, truly happy is when I'm on a stage."

"I was put on earth to make people laugh."

BARBRA STREISAND
1942–

Barbra Streisand is possibly one of the most famous stars in the world. For the first 20 or so years of her life, she is the only person who would have believed that was possible.

Raised in Brooklyn, New York, she was originally "Barbara" (with 3 *a*'s) but cut the second a as a teenager—to be different. Her father, Emanuel, died when she was a baby. And her mother, Diana, never really recovered from losing her husband and any kind of stability. Broke, with two young children to care for, Diana moved Barbra and her older brother, Sheldon, in with her parents. Crammed into the tiny one-bedroom apartment, Barbra would listen to her grandfather Louis Rosen singing Jewish prayers and songs. Though he was retired at the time, he had been a cantor.

Barbra went to the yeshiva on Willoughby Street in Flatbush, where her father had been a teacher. Though she was a very good student, the impression she made on her classmates was that of an oddly unattractive girl. As only kids can be, they were cruel and made fun of her large nose and a lazy eye that made her look cross-eyed. Scrawny and unable to afford stylish clothing, she was considered a *mieskeit* (Yiddish for "an ugly person").

When Barbra was seven, her mother married an abusive man with whom she had a baby daughter, Barbra's half-sister, Roslyn. Often singing in the hallways of her building on Pulaski Street or outside on the stoop, Barbra became known in the neighborhood as the girl with a good voice and no dad. She did not feel loved or supported by her mother but sought and found warm, kind mother figures elsewhere. An upstairs neighbor who cared for her also had a TV, which gave Barbra her first taste of what she would do when she grew up. "She wanted to become those people on the screen," her mother would say. From the time she was 14 and saw *The Diary of Anne Frank* on Broadway, Barbra was determined to perform on stage herself. Another upstairs neighbor in a different building would become a second family. She babysat for the Choy children and worked in the family's Chinese restaurant for four years, saving her wages to fund a summer apprenticeship at a theater in upstate New York.

Just shy of her 17th birthday, Barbra graduated a semester early from Erasmus High School in Brooklyn, eager to head across the East River to Manhattan. Sharing tiny midtown apartments with other struggling actors, taking acting classes, and auditioning, she was frustrated when casting directors didn't seem to appreciate her talent. Friends who heard her sing encouraged her to pursue musical roles instead of acting. Though Barbra was determined to be a serious actress, she also needed to eat. A close friend convinced her to compete in a talent contest to win a singing gig that included free dinners. With her spectacular voice, she easily won that job—and others. She started playing at a gay club called The Lion in Greenwich Village, becoming a hugely popular gay icon almost immediately. Then she moved on to bigger, more mainstream venues farther uptown. In one of those clubs, a young, hungry manager named Marty Erlichman saw her perform and was convinced she was the next big thing. Before she met Marty, she often heard agents, managers, and casting directors say that she was too Jewish looking. Her nose was too big. Her clothes were too kooky. Marty heard her voice, appreciated her humor, and thought she was just right. He wanted to manage her. (Sixty years later, they celebrated her seventh consecutive decade with a number one album.)

In 1961, when she was just 19—an age when many girls are just settling into college—Barbra had the audition that would change her life. She was cast in the Broadway musical *I Can Get It for You Wholesale*. The director, Arthur Laurents, wanted to cast her

immediately, but the producer, David Merrick, thought she was too ugly for the role. The powerful producer of blockbusters such as *Gypsy*, Merrick was ultimately convinced to give her a shot playing Miss Marmelstein. Those who expected Barbra to be grateful for her big break were surprised to find that she was regularly late to rehearsals, fought with the director, and changed her performance from show to show, throwing off the other actors. But when the show opened and audiences and critics saw Barbra in action, none of that mattered. She was mesmerizing. The show's leading man, Elliott Gould, became her boyfriend and later her husband. Before the end of the run, she had been cast as the lead in another Broadway musical, *Funny Girl*.

In just a few short years, Barbra had gone from singing for food to a sought-after star. And she was only just getting started. On October 1, 1962—after holding out for precisely the music deal she wanted—Barbra signed a recording contract with Columbia Records, the powerhouse label at the time. What's more, she and Marty had negotiated for full creative control. At the tender age of 20, her artistic vision was more important to her than up-front money, even though she had grown up in a home where every penny mattered. Though her mother had discouraged her and the entertainment world continued to question this mold-breaking talent, Barbra believed in herself. She knew she would make up for the smaller advance with her share of bigger sales—as long as she could control the finished product. This marked the beginning of decades of Barbra repeatedly, proudly insisting, "I'm in control of my own work," as if relinquishing that control was never an option. Her first album, *The Barbra Streisand Album*, made her the bestselling female vocalist of 1963 and remained in the Billboard Top 40 for 83 weeks. During this breakout year, Barbra was everywhere—making regular national TV appearances, performing for sold-out crowds at the fanciest night clubs, and even singing for President Kennedy.

After months on the road performing and promoting her album, she began rehearsals for *Funny Girl*, which was inspired by the life of Fanny Brice, a Jewish comedian and singer who also happened to have a big nose and a husband who gambled. Excited for the opportunity and challenge, Barbra faced a steep, stressful learning curve as the lead. Rehearsals and out-of-town tryouts were terrifying and difficult. But somehow it all came together, and on opening night, March 26, 1964, a few weeks before her 22nd birthday, a star was born.

The show was a huge success, and Barbra was living her childhood dream. But she didn't enjoy the repetitiveness of Broadway. "I liked the rehearsals. I loved changing scenes, changing things, songs, every night, change. But once they freeze it, that's it, you're in prison," she explained. She was eager to move on to other ventures. Fortunately, *Funny Girl*'s producers wanted to make a film adaptation, giving Barbra her big break into the movie business—and an Oscar and Golden Globe for Best Actress. Barbra was so busy and successful, she only took off time to give birth to her son, Jason, in 1966. The '60s and '70s were nonstop hit records and movies.

The world had never seen a movie star who looked, acted, and sounded like Barbra—ethnic, overtly Jewish, with a thick Brooklyn accent. With her crooked nose and close-set eyes, she defied traditional beauty norms as she seduced her handsome leading men and fans around the world.

She was also thrilled to bring interesting Jewish characters to the screen. After Fanny Brice, she played Dolly Levi in *Hello, Dolly!* (1969), Katie Morosky in *The Way We Were* (1973), Esther Hoffman Howard in *A Star Is Born* (1976), the title character in *Yentl* (1983),

> "I hope that I have succeeded in portraying Jewish people as I know them, in all their strength and diversity."

and Dr. Susan Lowenstein in *The Prince of Tides* (1991), exposing international audiences to strong, smart, complicated Jewish female characters. And the sheer force of her talent brought the world along with her, paving the way for a new type of woman whose beauty was nontraditional, who flaunted her Brooklyn accent and her Jewish roots, who was unapologetic about wanting things her way.

Captivating on screen, she was also uniquely positioned to reach legions of fans through multiple avenues—soundtracks, singles, and promotional appearances. The story and making of *Yentl*, in particular, exemplifies the force that is Barbra Streisand. First, it's about a young girl whose father dies and who then disguises herself as a boy to continue studying Torah. It wasn't exactly the stuff of a blockbuster. But the story of loss, inequality, and ambition (based on a short story by Isaac Bashevis Singer) was meaningful to Barbra. She threw her star power behind it, and then took on every role—producing, cowriting the screenplay, starring, directing, and producing the soundtrack—to complete her passion project. The movie made her the first woman ever to win a Golden Globe for Best Director.

> "I'm a Jewess through and through."

Like all good Jews, in the latter part of her career, she used her considerable money and influence to give back. As she explained in a 1995 speech at Harvard's John F. Kennedy School of Government, "Until women are treated equally with men, until gays and minorities are not discriminated against, until children have their full rights, artists must continue to speak out, and I will be one of them." She settled down with her second husband, James Brolin, in 1998, focusing more on her homes, gardens, dogs, and charitable causes—AIDS, women's health and equality, the environment, and a slew of Democratic political candidates. Of all of her many, many accomplishments and firsts as a singer, actor, director, producer, and icon, Barbra should also be credited for making it cool to be an outspoken, smart, tough, demanding, overtly proud Jewish woman.

SARAH SILVERMAN

1970 –

Sarah Silverman's hometown of Bedford, New Hampshire, has a population of 22,000, with all of its Jews apparently residing in her house. Her mother, Beth Ann, was a theater director. Her father, Donald, owned a clothing store and taught Sarah how to curse as soon as she could speak. They divorced when Sarah was six. Sarah then lived with her mom, and her three older sisters went to live with their father nearby. "We weren't really raised with any religion," she explains of her childhood in the very white, very Christian New England town. "We were just Jewish in that it oozed out of our pores."

There were occasional incidents of anti-Semitism (like the time a kid threw a fistful of change at Sarah's feet while she was getting on the school bus). Though she didn't feel actively hated in any way, she was conscious of being different. Dark and hairy in a blond, hairless gentile world. Sarah describes the survival skill honed by so many Jewish comedians and comedy writers over centuries of persecution: "Joking about my differentness seemed to put the people around me at ease. Even though I knew almost nothing about being a Jew other than that I *was* one." In addition to making people feel comfortable, disarming them with her self-deprecation, it also served as a form of defense. "The smart, fat kid will be the first to make a fat joke as protection from whatever insults the other kids might hurl at him, and as a smart Jew, I did likewise," she has explained.

Despite her parents' indifference to Judaism, it would play a major role in at least two of their four daughters' lives. Sarah's oldest sister, Susan, is a rabbi living in Israel. And it's fair to say that Sarah's spot-on observations of the quirks that differentiate members of the

tribe make her humor feel distinctly Jewish. This deep understanding of her people is evident in a viral video she produced for Barack Obama's 2008 presidential campaign called *The Great Schlep*. In it, she urges young Democrats to convince their Jewish grandparents in Florida to vote for Obama.

In her memoir, *The Bedwetter*, Sarah talks openly about not only the fact that she routinely wet her bed well into her teens but also how she suffered from deep depression during her adolescence. Like any loving Jewish parents, hers tried hard to find the right doctors for her ailments: a hypnotist for bedwetting, a psychiatrist who prescribed a load of Xanax, and another who eventually weaned her off medications. During that dark time, she remembers describing her feelings to her stepfather, saying, "I feel homesick," even though she was home. That feeling of aloneness stayed with her for years, during which she missed months of school at a time and found herself wondering why she couldn't just be happy like everyone else. She got out of bed, went to school (a new, smaller one), and started to function again, but depression would remain a part of her life.

When she was 18, Sarah left New Hampshire to attend New York University. When she moved into her NYU dorm in Greenwich Village, she could hardly believe that she was riding the subway, hanging out on the corner of West 3rd Street, handing out flyers for the Boston Comedy Club, where she also began to perform. A world away from Bedford, she no longer felt homesick. She had found her people: a circle of comedians, her NYU classmates, some actors. No shortage of Jews.

After her first year in college, her dad did something very unusual for a Jewish father: he agreed to pay her rent when Sarah said she wanted to drop out and focus on comedy. It turned out to be a smart gamble.

In 1993, she landed every comedy writer's dream job: a spot as writer and performer on *Saturday Night Live*. A year later, she was fired by fax. Next, she played a comedy writer on *The Larry Sanders Show* and then a fictionalized version of herself on her own show—*The Sarah Silverman Program*. A steady stream of film and TV roles, awards, comedy specials, fame, and fortune followed for the raunchy, outspoken, intellectual comedian. And then in 2018, Sarah's celebrity status was cemented with a star on the Hollywood Walk of Fame. Accepting the honor, she noted, "In a scary time when anti-Semitic crime is up 57 percent since 2016, it's not lost on me how lucky I am to be given a star and not have to sew it onto my clothes."

Yes, she went there. That's Sarah Silverman.

> "I don't think people really understand the value of happiness until they know what it's like to be in that very, very dark place. It's not romantic. Not even a little."

TIFFANY HADDISH

1979–

At Tiffany Haddish's bat mitzvah, she chanted a *parsha* (Torah portion) about Jacob from the Book of Genesis. In it, Jacob goes to sleep and has a dream about a ladder with angels ascending and descending it. God appears to him in the dream and promises to give Jacob and his descendants the land he was sleeping on. Jacob realizes that God was there even though Jacob hadn't known it. In her *d'var Torah* (a speech about her portion), Tiffany compared God's presence there to her own experience with Judaism, explaining to the friends, families, and celebrities who had gathered to celebrate her special milestone that she had always been Jewish—she just hadn't known it.

Some people are born to Jewish parents. Some people convert to Judaism. And some people reconnect with their father 24 years after being abandoned as a small child to discover that they are half-Jewish—and then embrace that discovery with zeal. That's what happened to Tiffany Haddish.

While most teenage Jewish girls learn about the bat mitzvah ritual in Hebrew school, preparing for their own special day, or by attending their friends' celebrations, Tiffany's exposure came through her weekend job in high school. She was an "energy producer" for a DJ who played at bar and bat mitzvahs all over the Los Angeles area. The DJ spotted Tiffany's exceptional energy at a school dance she attended, where he couldn't help but notice her leading the crowd on the dance floor. "Whenever I party, man, there's always a circle," she explains in her memoir, *The Last Black Unicorn*. The 18-year-old DJ, Tim, offered Tiffany a job doing what she did naturally: getting everyone around her to have a good time. She enjoyed this work for

"For a long time, I didn't even know Black Jews existed."

11 years and more than 500 bar and bat mitzvahs—until her acting and comedy career took off.

Getting dressed up to go dancing and working for a DJ would be a fun job for a lot of teenage girls. Tiffany *needed* that job though— she had to take care of herself from an early age. Her father pretty much disappeared when she was three. Her mom remarried and had four more children, and her grandmother would babysit when her stepfather wasn't around, which was often. Tiffany was so independent that one night when she was just nine years old, she insisted that she didn't need a babysitter, that she could make dinner and get her little brothers and sisters to bed, when it was time for her mom to leave for her work. So that night, with Tiffany in charge, her mother left for work. But she didn't come home.

Tiffany's mother had been in a terrible car accident on her way to work. She remained in the hospital for months, and when she did finally come home, she had serious brain damage. Not only was she incapable of caring for Tiffany and her brothers and sisters, but she became abusive as well. Tiffany and her siblings wound up in foster care for many painful, difficult years before they were able to move in with their grandmother. When Tiffany turned 18, her grandmother asked her to move out because she stopped receiving financial support from the state for Tiffany's care. Tiffany had to support herself, and the DJ gig was critical for her.

Homeless at times, with a family life that was unstable at best and deeply traumatic at worst, it's no wonder that Tiffany wanted to find her father. When she was 27, a cop boyfriend (whom she later married) helped track him down. Tsihaye Haddish was an immigrant from Eritrea (a country right next to Ethiopia, in the Horn of Africa). "My whole point to meet my father was just to know genetically what do I have to expect? And where the hell your a** been?" When her father told her that she was Jewish, Tiffany confirmed it with a DNA test from 23andMe and embraced her heritage. A practicing Jehovah's Witness up to that point, "I started learning more and more about the Torah. I could really relate to it."

Thirteen years later, on her 40th birthday, Tiffany became a woman according to Jewish tradition, on the very same day that Netflix released her comedy special *Black Mitzvah*. In her stand-up performances, in interviews, and in her memoir, Tiffany often talks about how she had to raise herself and learn things on the street. In foster care, she never knew whose home she was walking into and what they would be like. She struggled in school and faked her way through, barely able to read. It's understandable that she wanted to find out more about her roots, to feel a sense of belonging. She started to study Torah and traveled to Eritrea to meet her father's family. She explains this drive to reclaim her history in a broader context too: "Something that I feel like a lot of African Americans have been stripped of is their history. A lot of us don't know [our] origin. We don't know what our origin story is, because that was taken from us. And it talks about that in the Torah, I think it's so powerful."

In *Black Mitzvah*, after being carried to the stage on a chair while singing "Hava Nagila," Tiffany talks about her mitzvah, explaining that she's here to teach. Encouraging people to explore and embrace their heritage is just one of the lessons she has to share.

BLACK JEWS

Many of the Jews in Eritrea and Ethiopia came to those countries from Yemen, where they had lived for thousands of years. They made the trip across the Red Sea seeking economic opportunity, and there was a thriving Jewish community in Eritrea (and in neighboring Ethiopia) for hundreds of years. Then, to escape conflict between Ethiopia and Eritrea in the 1970s, many Eritrean Jews emigrated to Israel. In 1984 and 1985, thousands of Ethiopian Jews were airlifted to Israel in a rescue operation to escape famine during those years. With Jews now persecuted in Ethiopia and forbidden from practicing their religion in Eritrea, few Jews remain in the region.

NO-HOLDS-BARRED

ILANA GLAZER

1987–

UNAPOLOGETIC

ABBI JACOBSON

1984–

Ilana Glazer and Abbi Jacobson are not the first Jewish women to go into comedy. But they may be the first to unapologetically embrace their Judaism rather than mocking it.

Ilana describes herself as "a typical Reform girl. Had a bat mitzvah. Did my confirmation." She grew up in a town called St. James on eastern Long Island, a suburban-ish mix of farms and beach and Italian Catholic, Asian, and a few Jewish families. When Ilana was younger, she and her brother, Elliot (who is also a comedian), would write and perform sketch comedy at home and record everything using a camera provided by their parents. They would pretend they owned a TV station and film their own shows, something their grandfather had done before them on his own fake network, KRAP TV. Comedy was clearly in the genes.

When she graduated from high school, she followed her brother to New York University. The family had made many a weekend theater trip to the city, but actually living in a diverse and exciting place was a whole new experience for Ilana. (She even shared an apartment with *Crazy Ex-Girlfriend* star Rachel Bloom). While studying psychology at NYU, Ilana started to take improv (comedy improvisation) classes at Upright Citizens Brigade, a sketch-comedy group cofounded by Amy Poehler.

Abbi had a similar upbringing to Ilana's. She grew up in Wayne, New Jersey (where there were some but not many Jews), raised by an artist mom and graphic designer dad. (Her parents met at Camp Shalom.) The family belonged to a Reform synagogue where Abbi went to Sunday school and checked off the traditional Jewish girl milestones: summer camp, bat mitzvah, confirmation, and birthright trip. Abbi was passionate about both art and comedy from an early age. She took stand-up classes as a kid and then moved to New York City to pursue comedy after graduating from Maryland Institute College of Art. (Ironically, she partially supported her stand-up career with her art!)

One night in 2007, Ilana and Abbi were both at the Peter McManus Cafe with a bunch of other comedians looking to form an improv group. The only women in the group, they sat at the bar and got to know each other and fell madly in best-friend love. When Ilana asked Abbi if she was Jewish, she didn't believe her when she said she was. That was the night their lives would change.

They took classes together; did improv, stand-up, sketch comedy; wrote; catered; waitressed; and worked in a bakery (Abbi) and at

"I'm a total New York Jew. I can't believe you heard my voice, saw my face, and think I'm anything but a big old New York Jew." —ILANA

54

> "I'm not super, super religious. If this is okay to say, I'm more culturally Jewish." —ABBI

a Skinceuticals store (Ilana) and side by side making cold calls for a Groupon competitor called Lifebooker. They auditioned to be on a "house team" at Upright Citizens Brigade, which would have guaranteed them a weekly performance. But neither of them got the coveted spot. So in the fall of 2009, at a pizzeria on West 32nd Street in Manhattan, they decided to stop waiting for someone else to give them a chance. They brainstormed ideas for sketches and committed to make a web series together. They would write short episodes about their friendship, single life in New York City, things that annoyed them, and whatever else made its way into the notebooks that went everywhere with them. They named their series *Broad City*.

The friends wrote and performed, enlisting other friends to direct, costar, and film, and somehow they completed weekly five-minute episodes that they posted on YouTube and shared on social media. They hoped that their work might catch on, that maybe the web series would enable them to get writing or acting gigs someday. They went out on a limb and asked Amy Poehler to star in their web series finale. She said YES—and then, to their surprise and delight, she agreed to sign on as executive producer when they were heading out to Los Angeles to pitch the series to studios. This was a huge break for them—an endorsement from a comedy goddess. They sold a pilot to Fox, but after developing and then rewriting it for a year, Fox passed on the series. (Allegedly, executives found it "too girly.") But Comedy Central thought it was awesome and signed them. Ilana and Abbi had arrived.

"We were kids . . . all pretending to be producers, and then we really became producers," Ilana recalled in a documentary made during the final season. As creators/showrunners (the bosses on a TV series), they paved the way for *many* other women. They had felt the sting of sexism in the world of comedy, and once they had some influence, they wanted to make things more equitable. The cast and crew, extremely diverse and packed with women and brand-new talent, reflected their mission.

For five seasons of the TV series *Broad City*, Judaism played a starring role alongside Ilana and Abbi. Their characters first meet on a birthright trip! They eat bagels and break into "Hava Nagila." They attend Grandma Esther's shiva. They unsuccessfully fast (and discuss their guilt) on Yom Kippur. They board a subway car packed with Hassidim. Their dialogue is sprinkled with *oy*, *Adonai*, and casual Hebrew and yiddishisms. Ilana's character accessorizes with earrings emblazoned with the word *Jewess* and a gigantic Star of David necklace. They are also warm, open, neurotic, self-aware, and . . . familiar. Their characters' Jewishness is front and center at all times. The way Jewishness is.

EMMA LAZARUS EXTRAORDINARY ANNE FRANK FASCINATING RUTH WEST
VE JUDY BLUME GIFTED EMMA LAZARUS EXTRAORDINARY ANNE FRANK FAS
STHEIMER SUBVERSIVE JUDY BLUME GIFTED EMMA LAZARUS EXTRAORDINA
FASCINATING RUTH WESTHEIMER SUBVERSIVE JUDY BLUME GIFTED EMMA L
RDINARY ANNE FRANK FASCINATING RUTH WESTHEIMER SUBVERSIVE JUDY
EMMA LAZARUS EXTRAORDINARY ANNE FRANK FASCINATING RUTH WESTH
VE JUDY BLUME GIFTED EMMA LAZARUS EXTRAORDINARY ANNE FRANK FAS
STHEIMER SUBVERSIVE JUDY BLUME GIFTED EMMA LAZARUS EXTRAORDINA
FASCINATING RUTH WESTHEIMER SUBVERSIVE JUDY BLUME GIFTED EMMA L
RDINARY ANNE FRANK FASCINATING RUTH WESTHEIMER SUBVERSIVE JUDY
EMMA LAZARUS EXTRAORDINARY ANNE FRANK FASCINATING RUTH WESTH
VE JUDY BLUME GIFTED EMMA LAZARUS EXTRAORDINARY ANNE FRANK FAS
STHEIMER SUBVERSIVE JUDY BLUME GIFTED EMMA LAZARUS EXTRAORDINA
FASCINATING RUTH WESTHEIMER SUBVERSIVE JUDY BLUME GIFTED EMMA L
RDINARY ANNE FRANK FASCINATING RUTH WESTHEIMER SUBVERSIVE JUDY
EMMA LAZARUS EXTRAORDINARY ANNE FRANK FASCINATING RUTH WESTH
VE JUDY BLUME GIFTED EMMA LAZARUS EXTRAORDINARY ANNE FRANK FAS
STHEIMER SUBVERSIVE JUDY BLUME GIFTED EMMA LAZARUS EXTRAORDINA
FASCINATING RUTH WESTHEIMER SUBVERSIVE JUDY BLUME GIFTED EMMA L
RDINARY ANNE FRANK FASCINATING RUTH WEST   JUDY
EMMA LAZARUS EXTRAORDINARY ANNE FRANK   WESTH

WRITERS

VE JUDY BLUME GIFTED EMMA LAZARUS EXTRAORDINARY ANNE FRANK FAS
STHEIMER SUBVERSIVE JUDY BLUME GIFTED EMMA LAZARUS EXTRAORDINA
FASCINATING RUTH WESTHEIMER SUBVERSIVE JUDY BLUME GIFTED EMMA

EMMA LAZARUS
1849—1887

"Give me your tired, your poor,
Your huddled masses yearning to breathe free,
The wretched refuse of your teeming shore.
Send these, the homeless, tempest-tost to me,
I lift my lamp beside the golden door!"

— from "The New Colossus"

Emma Lazarus's famous poem "The New Colossus" was inscribed on a plaque that hangs inside the Statue of Liberty. She wrote the poem in 1883 to help raise funds to build the pedestal. These last lines are known throughout the world, along with Lady Liberty, for welcoming visitors and immigrants to New York Harbor, offering refuge and the promise of the American dream.

When Emma was alive, from 1849 to 1887, there were no airports. People traveled to America from other countries by boat. Millions of immigrants coming through the immigration station at Ellis Island were greeted by the statue and felt the power of Emma's words.

The Lazarus family lived that distinctly American dream. Her Sephardic ancestors emigrated from Portugal and were among the early Jewish settlers in America, arriving during the colonial era. Emma's parents, Moses and Esther Lazarus, were wealthy and educated. They made their fortune in the sugar-refining business. They were successful enough that they had a large home in New York City's Union Square and a summer mansion in Newport, Rhode Island. Emma and her six siblings were educated by private tutors. Emma was

a quick study with a gift for writing and language—she spoke Italian, French, and German. When she was 16, her father published a volume of her poetry and shared it with the writer Ralph Waldo Emerson, who became a mentor and friend.

In the early 1880s, Emma learned of the Russian pogroms and shifted her focus to advocating for the flood of refugees who began to arrive in New York. Her poems and essays published in magazines and newspapers spoke out forcefully about the persecution of Jews in Europe and the growing anti-Semitism in the United States and abroad. These events in Europe led her to argue for the creation of a Jewish homeland in Palestine.

Closer to home, she volunteered at the Hebrew Immigrant Aid Society and worked to provide services to poor Russian Jewish refugees. She helped establish the Hebrew Technical Institute in New York to provide vocational training to Jewish immigrants. Because she believed so deeply in America's principles of freedom, she was a forceful, passionate voice on behalf of Jews. Her words, welcoming the "tired and poor," were very much matched by her deeds on behalf of Jewish refugees.

SEPHARDIC JEWS

The first Jews to arrive in the American colonies were Sephardic—people with Spanish and Portuguese ancestry. The first Sephardic Jews came in 1654 to New Amsterdam (which would become New York) from Brazil. Over the next decades, Sephardic Jewish settlements were established in many other port cities including Newport, Philadelphia, Charleston, and Savannah.

ANNE FRANK
1929–1945

Anne Frank is possibly the best-known symbol of Jewish persecution, the most famous victim of anti-Semitism in the world. For the tens of millions of readers of *Diary of a Young Girl* (and millions more viewers of the movies or play inspired by her life), hers is the voice of the 6 million Jews killed during the Holocaust, 1.5 million of whom were children, like Anne.

Most people know at least part of Anne's story: She was born in Germany in 1929 just as Hitler was rising through the ranks of the Nazi Party. Things quickly became so difficult for Jews in Germany that Anne's parents, Otto and Edith, emigrated to Holland with their daughters—Margot, who was then seven, and Anne, who was four. There, things were better for Jews, at least for a few years: The girls could attend school in Amsterdam, where the family settled, and Otto was able to run a business selling pectin (a starch used to make jam), herbs, and spices.

But by May 1940, the German army had worked its way through Europe and occupied parts of the Netherlands as well. After their experience of extreme anti-Semitism in Germany, Otto had anticipated that things could get bad for Jews, and he prepared by converting the attic space above his business into a "Secret Annex." In early July 1942, several weeks after Anne received a diary for her 13th birthday and the day after Margot received a government summons demanding that she report to a work camp, the Franks told people they were emigrating to Switzerland. This was not true, because they couldn't get visas. Instead, they disappeared into their secret hiding place. They were joined in the small space by four

others: Otto's friend and business colleague, Hermann van Pels along with his wife and their son, Peter; and a dentist friend named Fritz Pfeffer. Otto's gentile employees cared for the group, bringing them food, books, and news of the outside world at tremendous risk to themselves.

Nearly every single day for the two years that they were in hiding, Anne wrote about her life. "When I write," she confides, "I can shake off all my cares. My sorrow disappears, my spirits are revived!" She was enormously gifted—had she lived in any other time, or had she survived, she would certainly have been known for her literary talent alone.

Sometimes, she writes about surprisingly ordinary teenage things—arguments with her mother, menstruation, or her feelings for Peter van Pels. Other entries are dark, sharing her constant fear of capture, concern for friends and neighbors who must be dead or suffering, and horror over the atrocities she witnessed from the attic window. On November 19, 1942, she reports, "In the evenings when it's dark, I often see long lines of good, innocent people accompanied by crying children, walking on and on, ordered about by a handful of men who bully and beat them until they nearly drop. No one is spared. The sick, the elderly, children, babies, and pregnant women— all are marched to their death."

On March 28, 1944, the spring before she was captured, Anne heard a radio broadcast asking all citizens to keep documentation and diaries in order to help write history after the war. Anne reread and began to revise her diary, while continuing to write in the hope that her account would be published. She mused, "Ten years after the war, people would find it very amusing to read about how we lived, what we ate and what we talked about as Jews in hiding."

On July 15, 1944, three weeks before they were arrested, Anne wrote what are perhaps the most cited lines of her diary: "It's a wonder I haven't abandoned all my ideals, they seem so absurd and impractical. Yet I cling to them because I still believe, in spite of everything, that people are truly good at heart." This expression of unimaginable optimism is immediately followed by far less sunny observations: "I see the world being slowly transformed into a wilderness, I hear the approaching thunder that, one day, will destroy us too, I feel the suffering of millions. . . . In the meantime, I must hold on to my ideals. Perhaps the day will come when I'll be able to realize them!" For the seven months following her arrest, that hope would be profoundly tested.

Anne's diary entries end abruptly on August 1, 1944. Her family was captured a few days later. They were taken from Amsterdam to Westerbork, a transit camp for Dutch prisoners. From there, on September 3, the Frank family was crammed onto a cattle car on a train packed with 1,015 other prisoners for an excruciating three-day journey—the final transport out of Westerbork to the deadliest concentration camp, Auschwitz-Birkenau, in Poland. There Anne, Margot, and their mother were separated from their father, sent to Women's Block 29. Half of the people on their transport—549 Jews, including every child under 15— were gassed to death the day after their arrival.

Conditions were abysmal at Birkenau, and Anne and Margot both contracted scabies (itchy sores and rashes caused by mites). They were sent to a scabies barracks, and Edith dug a hole under the wall to get food to her daughters. In October, the sisters were sent to Bergen-Belsen, separated from their mother who died 2 months later of starvation, exhaustion, and a broken spirit.

Margot became extremely ill at Bergen-Belsen. Though there were no gas chambers there, the camp was crowded, bitter cold, and teeming with typhus (a disease transmitted by lice). Anne's girlhood friend Hannah Kosler was already there when Anne arrived. Though their barracks were separated by a barbed wire fence, the girls managed to meet and talk through the fence a few times. Hannah was able to throw a small package of food to her dear friend, whom she later described as "a broken girl." By then, Anne's head was shaved and her frame was skeletal, her eyes sunken. "Anne told me 'I don't have any parents anymore.'" Anne was sure her father had been gassed on arrival at Auschwitz, explained Hannah. "I always think that if Anne had known her father was still alive, she might have had more strength to survive."

In March 1944, Margot fell out of the sisters' shared bunk bed, landing dead on the stone floor. Anne succumbed to typhus two days later—just weeks before the camp was liberated by Russian soldiers. She was 15.

> "It's difficult in times like these: ideals, dreams, and cherished hopes rise within us, only to be crushed by grim reality."

RUTH WESTHEIMER

1928–

You might not imagine that an Orthodox Jewish girl who grew up in Germany and fled the Nazis would spend her adult life talking about sex on an insanely popular radio show. But that is exactly what happened to Ruth Westheimer.

Born in Frankfurt, Germany, Karola Ruth Siegel was her parents' only child. Her father, Julius, had a successful business selling notions—buttons, ribbons, zippers, and the like. Her mother, Irma, had been a housekeeper for Julius's family before they married. They lived in a small ground-floor apartment in Frankfurt, on a block lined with red brick row houses. On Friday mornings, Karola would bring unbaked loaves of challah to the bakery, which would bake the loaves for her family since they didn't have an oven. In the evening, her father would take her to synagogue with him, stopping for an ice cream cone on the way. In her free time, the tiny, talkative girl loved to read, roller-skate, and go to the park with her grandmother, where they would often meet up with her cousins.

Like many Jews living peaceful, happy lives in Germany in the 1930s, the Siegel family had a hard time imagining that Hitler's rise and the wave of anti-Semitism that came with it would impact them—until it did.

On the night of November 10, 1938, during what's now known as Kristallnacht ("Night of Broken Glass"), 1,000 synagogues, 7,500 Jewish businesses, and thousands of homes were torched and destroyed. At least 91 Jews were killed, and thousands more were arrested. Later that same week, Karola's father was arrested by the SS, the German police, and sent to a labor camp. Six weeks later, on

January 5, 1939, ten-year-old Karola was sent to an Orthodox Jewish school in Switzerland to keep her safe. She did not want to leave Germany, but her father had sent a postcard insisting that she go, and her mother promised her that she would have the best chocolate in Switzerland and would reunite with her parents soon. There was no choice—she boarded the train.

> "My parents actually gave me life twice: Once when I was born, and once when they sent me to Switzerland."

The school was near a farm, surrounded by meadows, and it would have been a pleasant place under different circumstances. Friendly and upbeat, Karola made the most of a desperate situation. Though only the boys were allowed to go to the village school, one of them shared his books with Karola. She got her hands on a book called *Letters for Young Girls* and taught herself and then her friends about menstruation and sex from its pages. For the first year, Karola and her parents sent letters back and forth. But in September 1941, the letters stopped. She turned 12, 13, 14, 15, and finally 16 at the school, without word from her family.

After Nazi Germany surrendered to the Allies in May 1945, the school (which had transformed into an orphanage) received a list of the names of students' family members who had survived. The Siegels were not on the list. With nobody and nothing to return to in Frankfurt, Karola set off for what was then British-controlled Palestine with some of her friends. The teenagers

KINDERTRANSPORT

In the nine months following Kristallnacht, the British government arranged to take in nearly 10,000 German Jewish refugee children. Many had been, or would be, orphaned when their parents were sent to concentration camps. Ruth was one of just several hundred children who were sent to countries other than England.

took a train to Marseille, France, where Karola saw the ocean for the first time. On the way to her new, postwar life, she was told that the name Karola sounded too German. From then on, she would go by her middle name, Ruth.

In Palestine, Ruth lived on several kibbutzim (communal farms). She joined Haganah, the Jewish defense force. Unusually tiny at 4 feet 7 inches tall, she was trained as a sniper and scout. It was an exciting but dangerous life—her foot was nearly blown off at one point during the 1948 Israeli War of Independence. Like many Jewish refugees at the time, Ruth had fled persecution in one country only to have to fight for her life in her new home.

By 1950, she was ready to focus on the education she'd been robbed of as a child. She went to Paris, where she studied and then taught psychology. Six years later, she emigrated to New York City and earned a master's degree in sociology while teaching herself English by reading romance novels. Along the way, she had a daughter, Miriam (marrying, then divorcing her French father). As a single mom, she met Manfred Westheimer, another Jewish refugee, on a ski weekend in the Catskill Mountains. They fell in love, married, and had a son named Joel. After decades of being unsettled, Ruth had a permanent home and a family to love—and to love her.

With an insatiable thirst for knowledge, Ruth continued her studies, earning her doctorate in education at Columbia University in 1970. She was now a highly educated woman, fluent in German, French, Hebrew, and English, and ready to teach for real. She worked at Planned Parenthood, educating women about contraception. And for many years, she researched and trained with Helen Singer Kaplan, a pioneering sex therapist. Ruth's unique teaching style was surprisingly inspired by her Orthodox upbringing. "In the Talmud, it says that a lesson taught with humor is a lesson retained," she explains. "I came from an Orthodox Jewish home so sex for us Jews was never considered a sin." Sex is treated in a very practical, proscribed way according to Jewish law. Ruth had two important things going for her: First, she had always been completely comfortable talking about all things sexual. Second, and most importantly, Ruth was determined to celebrate pleasure as an adult— perhaps because of, or in spite of, her tragic childhood.

This straightforward yet exuberant approach to sex combined with her memorable accent and an infectious laugh turned out to be a magical formula. In 1980, she was invited to do an interview on a public affairs show on local radio station WNYW. She was so compelling that the station managers decided to give "Dr. Ruth" her own show. Concerned about censors, *Sexually Speaking* originally aired on Sunday nights at midnight so as not to attract too much attention. Her audience found her anyhow. Over the next two years, the show expanded to two hours, during which she captivated millions of listeners each week. The show was syndicated all over the country as Dr. Ruth and her unique voice became famous. Appearing on late-night and talk shows, publishing bestselling books, even hosting her own TV shows, the beloved sex expert was also a forceful advocate for safe sex and abortion rights.

Dr. Ruth still lives in the three-bedroom apartment in Washington Heights that she moved into when she first came to New York City and the neighborhood was populated with Jewish immigrants. International fame and success have not changed the person known to her four grandchildren as Omi and around the world as Dr. Ruth. She remains both a humble refugee and an astonishing success story.

Dr. Ruth has talked about how German Jews never cry in public. While she maintains a happy outward appearance in her career as a superstar sex expert, she has also taken on the role of educating people about the Holocaust. As she explained to Reuters in a 1995 interview, "Every time I am sad I just have to think about my five-year-old grandson. Hitler didn't want me to have that grandson. I put the picture of my grandson in my mind and say—You see, we did triumph." Living a joyful, successful life is her personal and public triumph—though it is only part of Dr. Ruth's story.

JUDY BLUME

1938–

The "people of the book" have spawned many successful, famous Jewish writers. But few authors have been embraced by generation after generation like Judy Blume has. For women who read books such as *Are You There God? It's Me, Margaret*; *Deenie*; and *Starring Sally J. Freedman as Herself* when they were first published in the 1970s, the subjects of her books were considered really racy. Nobody was talking about divorce, menstruating, puberty, or religion in books for middle schoolers back then.

Culturally and spiritually Jewish, though not very religious, Judy Blume's Jewish characters resemble her. "Sally is the kind of kid I was at ten," Judy has said of Sally J. Freedman. Her characters are regular girls growing up in the suburbs, much like Judith Sussman did before she became bestselling author Judy Blume. She spent her childhood in Elizabeth, New Jersey, where everyone was Jewish or Christian. She attended Sunday school and way too many boisterous shivas for her father's six siblings, all of whom died by the time they were 60. She met and married her first husband, John Blume, while she was a student at New York University and then had two children, one after the other, when she graduated.

Judy, who has always had a vivid imagination and what she describes as "stories inside my head," found young motherhood stifling. "I was just losing it until I found my way with creative work," she has said. She went back to NYU to study creative writing, and the first several years of her career were marked mainly by rejection letters from publishing houses.

> "I was shy, I was fearful. But when it came to writing, somehow I became fearless and that changed my life."

And then in 1969, her first book, a picture book called *The One in the Middle Is the Green Kangaroo*, was published. A year later, *Are You There, God? It's Me, Margaret* came out, making Judy Blume a household name. The relatable, beloved half-Jewish, half-Christian character's conversations with God mirror Judy's own conversations, Blume has said. "I would plead, 'Just let me be normal,' which meant let me have my period, give me some breasts, and hurry up."

The character that gives the most insight into Judy Blume is Sally J. Freedman, who, according to Judy, "explains how, even why I became a writer." *Starring Sally J. Freedman as Herself* (published in 1977) is set in Miami in 1947, just a few years after World War II ended. In it, Sally has just moved, and, in addition to worrying about boys and being popular in her new school, she is also partly convinced that her new neighbor is Hitler in disguise. Judy was seven when the war ended, and though she was somewhat removed from the danger in Elizabeth, New Jersey, the threat of the Holocaust, the whispering between adults, the anxiety around such a monumental event was still felt in some ways in a Jewish home. "I knew that he'd wanted to kill all the Jews in the world. And I was a Jew," Judy describes her understanding of Hitler when she was little. As she attempted to connect the dots as a child, she feared that maybe the Holocaust could happen again. She compares Sally's fictional world to her world as a child: "a world of secrets kept from children, a world of questions without answers."

In sharing the stories in her head, exploring the fears and hopes of regular kids who were unraveling the secrets of the grownups in their lives, Judy Blume has published dozens of books that have sold more than 85 million copies all around the world. And she has spent

her career fighting the parents, teachers, and librarians who have sought to ban her books from school libraries. Judy never intended to be controversial when tackling her subjects; she just talked about the stuff that was in her head, and in many cases, that turned out to be the stuff that was on kids' minds. She put taboo subjects out in the open, and in doing so, brought comfort, connection, and happiness to generations of girls.

The honesty in her writing, the owning of neuroses, the eagerness to discuss things that many people would not openly discuss is so very Jewish. The fact that so many writers now bare their souls without pretension or fear is in large part thanks to Judy Blume's example.

ARTISTS

SONIA DELAUNAY
1885–1979

When Sara Stern was born, the youngest of three children, her parents struggled to support the family in Ukraine. By the time she was five years old, her parents sent her to live with her mother's wealthy brother, Henri Terk, a Jewish lawyer in St. Petersburg, Russia. Henri and his wife Anna could not have children of their own. They treated Sara as if she were their daughter and eventually adopted her, at which point she changed her name to Sonia Terk. The arrangement worked out well for all of them.

St. Petersburg was a sophisticated city with lots of art and culture. Many Jews lived there because it was more tolerant than other Russian cities, particularly for affluent Jews. Sonia was able to go to a good school. She traveled throughout Europe with her aunt and uncle, spending summers in Finland. One of her teachers noticed that she had artistic talent, so when she was 18, her uncle sent her to the Academy of Fine Arts in Karlsruhe, Germany. Exposed to many European artists at the school, she decided to move to Paris in 1905 to study at the Académie de la Palette. There she was exposed to early Fauvists, whose intense colors influenced her own sensibility. At that time, major young artists including Henri Matisse and Pablo Picasso were living and working in Paris. It was very much the center of the modern art world, and Sonia was right there in the thick of it. She preferred spending her time in galleries rather than classes, and as she wandered through the cobblestoned streets of Paris, she saw paintings by Matisse and Picasso, Henri Rousseau, Paul Gauguin, and others.

In 1908, she married a gallery owner and friend, Wilhelm Uhde. It was not a marriage based in love. Wilhelm was gay, and it wasn't

acceptable to be openly gay in the early 1900s. With a wife, nobody questioned his sexuality. For Sonia, it wasn't really acceptable for a young woman to be living on her own. Marrying Wilhelm enabled her to live away from her family in the city she loved. Being married also meant that she would receive her dowry (an allowance from her aunt and uncle in Russia). Wilhelm held a show for Sonia in his gallery, and he introduced her to his other artist friends, including the man who would become her next husband, Robert Delaunay. In 1910, she divorced Wilhelm (amicably) and married Robert. They had a son, Charles, the following year.

Robert and Sonia were both intrigued by color and the way in which colors look different depending on the colors near them. This was something they studied and experimented with. Their style of painting, overlapping vivid colors and shapes, was called orphism. They later took it one step further—simultaneously contrasting colors—a theory Robert called simultanism.

Sonia cared less about the theory and more about making things. She decided to sew a quilt for Charles made of colorful fabric scraps, like those she'd seen in the homes of Russian peasants. She noticed that the overlapping patches of fabric evoked a concept similar to what she and Robert were doing in their experimental paintings. It occurred to her that art did not have to be limited to paint on canvas, a realization that led to the next stage in her career.

She started to design fabric, furniture and clothing, boxes and books, cushions, and collages. Though critics, galleries, and museums might differentiate between fine art and decorative arts, Sonia believed that all of it was art. "For me there is no gap between my painting and my so-called 'decorative' work. I never considered the 'minor arts' to be artistically frustrating; on the contrary, it was an extension of my art," she explained.

In 1914, she and Robert were traveling in northern Spain when World War I broke out, so they decided to stay put, settling in Iberia for close to seven years. There she opened a design store called Casa Sonia. She was able to incorporate her Ukrainian roots into her fabric arts. She described childhood memories of pure, vivid colors, "memories of peasant weddings in my country in which the red and green dresses decorated with many ribbons, billowed in dance."

When they returned to Paris in 1920, she turned her wearable art into a big business. Her designs— boldly patterned scarves, poem dresses, and striking textiles—appeared in the best stores around the world, and her artwork started to hang in galleries and museums. She also designed costumes and sets for operas, ballets, films, and plays. Sonia and Robert's apartment became another canvas. She designed all of their furniture and rugs and painted their walls, and they often hosted writers and artists and thinkers in this creative lair.

Her charmed life ground to a halt in the early 1940s. When Germany invaded France, Sonia and Robert moved to the South of France. Robert died shortly thereafter in 1941. Sonia was heartbroken and turned her attention to sealing his legacy, ensuring that his work was remembered and exhibited. She also worried about evading capture during World War II, concerned that her Jewish identity would be revealed.

In 1964, she became the first living female artist to have a retrospective exhibition (covering all the different eras of her career) at the Louvre (one of the most important museums in the world) in Paris. She continued to make art and influence others until she died at the age of 94. She will be remembered for her abstract circle paintings, for her spectacular textiles, and for always thinking ahead of the curve—and pulling others along with her.

THE GOD OF BEAUTY

Sonia was not a practicing Jew. She played down her Judaism in order to live a rich and productive artistic life at a time when Jews faced oppression and persecution. She found her own kind of spirituality outside of religion. As she described it, "For a very long time I hadn't believed in God, but I would seek out nature, and I felt the need to fulfill my desires. . . . Praying to beauty—there is a great deal of selflessness in that, and a purely aesthetic element which alone ennobles life and makes it love."

DIANE ARBUS
1923—1971

By all appearances, Diane Nemerov had a really nice life growing up in New York City. Her maternal grandfather, a Russian immigrant named Frank Russek, had founded a very successful fur store. When her parents, Gertrude and David Nemerov, married, David started to manage the store and helped expand it into a department store that sold luxury clothing on Manhattan's Fifth Avenue. Diane; her older brother, Howard; and her younger sister, Renee, went to private schools, were cared for by nannies, and grew up on the very upscale Central Park West in Manhattan. When their nanny took them to the playground, they wore their white gloves in the sandbox.

Many people would envy her posh lifestyle, but as an adult, Diane saw all of this privilege as a problem. "I never felt adversity. I was confirmed in a sense of unreality which I could only feel as unreality. That sense of being immune was ludicrous as it seems a painful one." She also suffered from depression, as did her mother. Her mother's bouts of depression meant that she wasn't very involved with Diane and her siblings. Her father was distracted by work.

With distant parents, Diane and her siblings became very close and were also extremely artsy. Her brother became the US poet laureate, and her sister became a painter and sculptor. Diane dabbled in painting in high school as well but talked about hating the sound of the brush on canvas.

She met her husband, Allan Arbus, when she was 14 years old and he worked in the art department at Russeks. They had a somewhat secret romance until they were married by a rabbi when she was 18. Allan was Diane's introduction to the world of photography. He gave

"A photograph is a secret about a secret. The more it tells you, the less you know."

Diane her first camera and turned their bathroom into a darkroom. While he went off to serve in World War II, she photographed her pregnancy and the birth of their first daughter, Doon. In 1946, after he returned from the war and after she had worked in the advertising department at Russeks, they launched a commercial photography business. Diane would art direct and style their shoots, and Allan would shoot and develop the film, refining the prints. Russeks hired them for their first job, and they were quickly working steadily for major fashion magazines like *Vogue* and *Harper's Bazaar*.

She had a glamorous job and traveled to interesting places, but Diane didn't find fashion photography gratifying. After their second daughter, Amy, was born, Diane began to study with an influential photographer named Lisette Model and eventually left the business she'd started with her husband. When they separated in 1959, Diane moved to Westbeth Artists Community (affordable housing for artists) in Manhattan's west village and began to explore creatively.

Despite her privileged upbringing and a stylish career as a fashion photographer, Diane seemed to seek out discomfort, outsiders, and what she referred to as "freaks" in order to find herself, an

A JEWISH GIANT AT HOME WITH HIS PARENTS

One of Diane's most famous photographs is of a Jewish man named Eddie Carmel, who suffered from gigantism. Born in Israel, Eddie and his parents immigrated to the US when he was a boy. He made a career out of his height—all 8 feet 9 inches of it. He and Diane met when he was performing at Hubert's Dime Museum and Flea Circus in New York City's Times Square. In the famous photo she shot in 1970, he is hunched over and supported on canes, still towering over his parents in their living room in the Bronx.

outsider in her own way. She went to Times Square and Coney Island, where she befriended and eventually photographed tattooed men, sword swallowers, and snake dancers. She went to gay nightclubs and photographed female impersonators. She photographed families at nudist camps and children in Central Park. She took many famous photographs of twins. She photographed people who were sick, dying, and dead—including her father. She seemed to be always highlighting, questioning, and challenging identity, and in doing so developed a distinct style. She described her photographs as capturing "the space between who someone is and who they think they are."

Most often, she would get to know her subjects quite well before she photographed them so that they would open up to her. In her black-and-white photos, her subjects are looking directly at her or at the camera. Her work is eerie, unforgettable, and also controversial. She explained that her subjects "made me feel a mixture of shame and awe." But she seemed to revere them as well, elaborating that "people go through life dreading they'll have a traumatic experience. Freaks were born with their trauma. They've already passed their test in life. They're aristocrats."

She began to teach photography, too, and told her students, "The thing that's important to know is that you never know. You're always sort of feeling your way." Still a work in progress, by 1970, she was on her way to becoming world famous. Along with the Museum of Modern Art, which showcased her work, she had elevated photography to the level of fine art. While many museums, critics, and collectors regarded her then, and now, as a genius, others criticized her for exploiting her subjects. One of her final projects, a series of photographs of people with intellectual disabilities taken at a home in Vineland, New Jersey, is particularly troubling for this reason.

Toward the end of her life, she was sick with hepatitis and had fallen into a deep depression. Psychiatric medications were far less sophisticated and effective then and Diane's struggle with depression and intense mood swings was ongoing. She committed suicide in July 1971, leaving a mysterious body of work for others to interpret.

HELEN FRANKENTHALER

1928–2011

elen Frankenthaler was the youngest of three daughters in a privileged New York City family. Her father, Alfred, was a well-respected New York State Supreme Court judge. Her mother was a striking, elegant German Jewish immigrant. The family belonged to Temple Emanu-El, the opulent synagogue founded by New York City's uptown German Jews, and the girls all went to exclusive private schools. Helen played at the playground behind the Metropolitan Museum of Art, eight blocks from her family's Park Avenue home. Life was pretty charmed for Helen until her father died when she was 12. He had always made her feel loved and special, and when he died after a months-long illness, she suffered from migraine headaches and anxiety for several years.

This happened about the same time the Nazis began rounding up Jews in Germany. Though Helen may not have realized it at the time, her mother and other family members were trying to help their relatives who were still trapped in Germany. Unable to escape, two of her cousins drowned themselves, and her mother's uncle overdosed on sleeping pills in September 1942, rather than board the train to a concentration camp.

While the war raged in Europe, Helen was sent to Brearley, a girls' school that limited the number of Jews who could attend. She failed two years in a row due to what had become overwhelming anxiety. She transferred to the Dalton School, where a beloved art teacher,

Mexican painter Rufino Tamayo, helped turn things around for her. He restored her confidence and taught her technique and even how to mix her own paints from tubes of pigment, linseed oil, and turpentine.

From Dalton, Helen went to Bennington College, which was then a women's school and known for its fine art program and bohemian student body. The rigorous art program focused on cubism, and Helen thrived there. She was friends with Groucho Marx's daughter Miriam. Another close friend, Gaby Rodgers, had been a classmate of Anne Frank's in Amsterdam before emigrating to the US. Helen moved back to New York City, ready to become an artist. Thanks to an inheritance from her father, she would not be a starving artist. She was able to move into her own apartment with a college friend and rent a studio as well, all without having to give up expensive haircuts.

In the spring of 1950, Helen was asked to curate a show of art by Bennington graduates for a New York City gallery. She invited an influential art critic, Clement Greenberg, and he came to the show. He was not a fan of Helen's attempt at cubism, but he was charmed by Helen. The two began a five-year romantic relationship (in spite of their 20-year age difference). He introduced her to all of the stars in the exploding New York art scene: Jackson Pollock and Willem de Kooning (both of whom became famous abstract expressionists) and the acclaimed sculptor David Smith, among others. They regularly socialized with established Jewish writers and intellectuals as well. Greenberg undoubtedly opened many doors and made connections for Helen, and she had detractors because of it. But it was her sheer talent and drive that sustained her.

Greenberg suggested she study with Hans Hofmann in Provincetown, Massachusetts, and she listened. When she returned to New York City afterward, "Work was pouring out of me, painting after painting," she reflected. "I had so many ideas I couldn't get them out quickly enough." She surrounded herself with artists—many older and more established—who pushed, inspired, and supported her. There were dinners at Greenberg's, drinks at a Greenwich Village bar, and sometimes the group would get together at her building, which had a swimming pool.

Helen credited Jackson Pollock's work with transforming her as an artist. Greenberg took her to a gallery show in 1951; it was the first time she'd seen Pollock's mural-sized, explosive drip paintings. She described that powerful moment in this way: "I wanted to live in this land, and I had to live there but I just didn't know the language." It wasn't that Helen suddenly realized she wanted to make drip paintings. She simply felt freed. For her, Pollock's work "opened up what one's own inventiveness could take off from . . . to be free with what you are making that comes out of you." It was then that she began to paint on the floor, as Pollock did. The act of painting became more intimate for her, and the boundaries of the canvas disappeared. She would pour paint onto the canvas, using brushes, rollers, sponges, and her hands to manipulate the paint, walking around and even onto the canvas as she worked.

In 1950, she was invited to exhibit in a prestigious show titled *15 Unknowns*, where she showed a work called *Beach* that was made from coffee grounds, oil, sand, and plaster of Paris. Less than a year after she encountered Pollock, just before her 23rd birthday, she had her first solo show at the Tibor de Nagy Gallery. She was no longer an unknown but on her way.

A year later, she decided to try something completely new. On October 26, 1952, she entered her studio and laid a canvas on the floor. Rather than priming her canvas (covering it with a layer of paint mixed with glue, which prevents colors from bleeding and also enables an artist to scrape off a mistake), she decided to paint directly on the canvas. She thinned her paint with turpentine. She drew some lines in charcoal. And then she began to pour. Blue, pink, peach, seafoam green, and red. She watched the colors soak into the canvas and pool, as the shapes of the Nova Scotia coast she had visited that summer emerged. And when she was done, she had created her first masterpiece, *Mountains and Sea*. In doing so, she had invented her signature method of "soak staining" the canvas. This novel technique inspired other artists and is considered to be the bridge to the next art movement—color field painting.

> "When the artist reveals his concern for the audience, there is something wrong, something cynical, and the creative process is no longer pure."

Though Helen's art career was going well, her relationship with her moody, critical boyfriend was not. She broke up with Greenberg and in late 1957 started to date another very successful abstract painter, Robert Motherwell. They married four months after their first date, in the spring of 1958 (and divorced in 1971). He also came from a wealthy family, and there was a lot of resentment of the "golden couple" by the financially struggling artist community. They influenced and supported one another, traveling to France and Spain for a long honeymoon, where they spent time exploring ancient cave paintings.

In the 1960s, Helen switched from oil to acrylic paints and achieved the next status level as an artist. She had her first museum show in 1960, a retrospective at the Jewish Museum in New York City. In 1969, she had another major retrospective at the Whitney Museum of American Art, also in New York City. She began to experiment with printmaking, sculpture, woodcuts, and other media, constantly exploring, looking for new ways to express herself. She continued to show in major museums and galleries around the world, making art until she died. The paintings of her later years reflect more of the greens and blues she would have seen from her Connecticut studio that overlooked Long Island Sound.

LEE KRASNER

There was one other woman, a Jewish woman, in the circle of abstract expressionists who were Helen's original mentors and community: Lee Krasner. Lee was 20 years older than Helen, part of the first generation of abstract expressionists. She may be best known for being married to the artist Jackson Pollock, but she was an accomplished artist in her own right. The daughter of Russian Jewish immigrants, her most famous works include her Little Image series of 31 small paintings, collages crafted from her own and Pollock's discarded canvases, and large, vibrant paintings inspired by nature.

SCIENTISTS

ANNA FREUD
1895–1982

The father of psychoanalysis, Sigmund Freud, was also the father of Anna Freud. She, in turn, was the founder of child psychoanalysis.

Born in Vienna, Austria, the youngest of six children, Anna was extremely close to her father. She did not have a good relationship with her mother and siblings, however. She was particularly competitive with her sister Sophie, who was two and a half years older, considered quite beautiful, and her mother Martha's favorite. When Anna finished high school, she began working as an elementary school teacher and was regarded as an outstanding educator. She loved working with children and was known to get down on the floor and play with her students. When she was 15 years old, Anna started attending her father's lectures and also sat outside his library listening to his discussions with visitors. Sigmund felt that Anna could learn more at home than in college, and that was probably true in her unique household. The field of psychoanalysis was forming before her eyes and ears.

A group of mostly Jewish men in Vienna, led by Sigmund Freud, was essentially inventing psychotherapy at the time. Working as a neurologist earlier in his career, Freud decided that mental illness was the result of keeping thoughts inside and repressing them. He believed if people talked about their memories, their fears, dreams, and secrets, that they could heal. The method he practiced and popularized was psychoanalysis. One way someone trained as an analyst was to undergo psychoanalysis herself. In 1918, at the age of 23, Anna began four years of treatment with her father. Today, a family member would never treat another family member or even a friend. It's actually forbidden as unethical. Talking about your most personal secrets, fears, and fantasies with your father would probably be, at the very least, really awkward and possibly damaging. But Anna did just that. Her relationship with her father was intense and strange, yet central to everything she did with her life.

In 1919, during the First World War, she began volunteering at the Baumgarten Children's Home, which provided education, food, and shelter to Viennese Jewish war orphans. This was the first of many experiences that combined charitable work with the chance to observe and help children in need. Anna had so much experience compressed into so few years that, by 1923, she was running her own practice treating children *and* teaching at the Vienna Psychoanalytic Training Institute—the center of psychoanalysis. She rose through its ranks over the next 15 years.

> "Sometimes the most beautiful thing is precisely the one that comes unexpectedly and unearned."

Whereas a lot of Sigmund Freud's work focused on helping adults to process childhood memories, Anna focused on helping children to access their emotions. Her extensive work first with children and then with adolescents taught her that the approach to children's therapy needed to be very different than the way someone worked with adults. Recognizing how brilliant Anna was, her father urged her to make time for her studies and career before she married. Whether she was following his advice or simply wasn't interested in men, Anna never married or had children of her own. She did, however, continue the family tradition of treating relatives, refining her method by analyzing her nephew Ernst (whose mother, Sophie, had died of the Spanish flu). Anna helped him to overcome his fear of the dark. (Many years later, Ernst grew up to become a psychoanalyst as well.) Anna also treated all four children of her close friend Dorothy Burlingham, children she helped raise when Dorothy became her life partner. Dorothy saw Sigmund Freud for her own analysis. It was all pretty complicated in the Freud-Burlingham households.

Together, in the winter of 1937, the two women opened the Jackson Nursery in Vienna, a charitable center that was funded by an American psychoanalyst and friend named Edith Jackson. Run by Anna and Dorothy, the center provided free childcare and food for poor babies and toddlers. It also became a testing ground for Anna's theories about child behavior. Among other things, she studied feeding patterns, noting that given the choice of what to eat and when, toddlers would independently balance their own eating schedule.

While all of the cutting-edge work going on in the field of psychoanalysis in 1930s Vienna was making the world a more enlightened place, the Nazis were rapidly spreading hate and exerting their influence over Europe. In 1938, they annexed Austria, and almost overnight it became a very unsafe place to be Jewish. There were reports of Jews being beaten in the streets while their gentile neighbors watched. Though they were not religious Jews, the Freuds were undeniably Jewish—and very well known. Anna and her father were interrogated by the Gestapo (the German police) and permitted to go only after Sigmund agreed to sign a statement saying that they had been treated well by the Gestapo.

Fortunately, the Freuds were well connected and had friends who could make necessary payments and arrangements to get them safely out of Vienna and to London. While caring for her father (who died of cancer the next year), Anna was able to set up a private practice there and published what remains a definitive book, *The Ego and Mechanisms of Defense*. This book introduced the concept of defense mechanisms, or tools that children (and adults) use to protect themselves when they are in danger. *Denial* (refusing to admit there's a problem) and *regression* (blaming others and evading responsibility) are two of the now-familiar behaviors she explored in the book. This transformative idea of defense mechanisms—that we act in certain ways to protect ourselves from internal and external forces—was first put into words, understood, and treated by Anna.

WHAT HAPPENED TO THE JEWS IN AUSTRIA?

Before World War II, the 192,000 Jews living in Austria represented about 4 percent of Austria's population. Most of them, like the Freuds, lived in Vienna. On March 12, 1938, the Nazis marched into Vienna to cheering crowds. In response to intense Nazi propaganda, the Austrian people overwhelmingly voted to be annexed by Germany. Jews and Gypsies (or Roma) were not permitted to vote. In November of that year, Kristallnacht pogroms destroyed synagogues and Jewish businesses in Vienna, and thousands of Jews were arrested and sent to concentration camps. Many—117,000—emigrated to other countries over the next year. Starting in October 1941, about 65,000 Jews were deported to ghettos or concentration camps throughout eastern Europe, and many were killed. The remaining Jews, around 7,000, were in hiding or married to gentiles.

Dorothy had relocated to London with Anna, and together they established the Hampstead War Nurseries to provide foster care for children during the war. There Anna was able to observe the impact of separation from their families on children's development. After the war, a group of young children who survived Theresienstadt, a ghetto in what is now the Czech Republic, arrived at Hampstead. For six years, she worked closely with them, also studying the impact of war and trauma on children. After decades of treating hundreds of children, in 1952 she opened the Hampstead Clinic, a research and training center devoted to child analysis. The first generation of child psychotherapists was trained in Anna's center!

As a Jewish woman living in Europe in the 1900s, Anna was uniquely positioned to observe and support children during and after the trauma of two world wars. The idea of openly talking about emotions also appears to be very Jewish (and not mere coincidence that the field of psychotherapy was launched largely by Jews). A history of persecution and the experience of the Holocaust at that particular moment in time also brought Jewish suffering to the forefront. And there, in the heart of it all, was Anna Freud, who made an extraordinary mark in terms of our understanding and treatment of children's mental and emotional health.

ANNA AND DOROTHY

Dorothy Tiffany Burlingham was an American heiress. Her paternal grandfather, Charles, founded Tiffany & Co., the high-end jewelry design company, and her father, Louis, became known for his stained-glass lamps. Dorothy fled an abusive husband in the US and went to Vienna, Austria, with her children, in part to work with Sigmund Freud. She developed a close, lifelong friendship and partnership with Anna, as she, too, became an analyst, coauthored books with Anna, and worked alongside her in many of her ventures. They lived together as a family, and many scholars now look back and think that they may have been lovers as well. But because they lived in a pre-LGBTQ pride era, and also because Anna's relationship with her own sexuality was deeply affected by years of analysis with her father, it's not entirely clear.

GERTRUDE ELION

1918 – 1999

For a Jewish girl whose family valued education, it was very frustrating for Gertrude Elion not to be able to complete her PhD. But sexism and life got in the way.

Gertrude was born in Manhattan and then her family moved to the Bronx, which, in 1918, was a very Jewish, suburban-like neighborhood in New York City. The Bronx Zoo, with hundreds of rolling green acres, was her playground. Her dad, a dentist, had emigrated from Lithuania, and her mom came to the US from an area of Russia that is now part of Poland. She was so smart that she skipped two grades and graduated from high school at age 15. And that is when the defining trauma of her life occurred: her grandfather died a quick and painful death from stomach cancer.

It was so hard for Gertrude to see her grandfather suffer that, as she headed off to NYC's Hunter College, she was determined to study chemistry and dedicate her life to finding a cure for cancer. At Hunter, there were many other female students studying science, but most of them planned to teach when they graduated. Gertrude's family had lost most of their money in the 1929 stock market crash. Fortunately Hunter was free for students who had strong enough grades, but Gertrude could not get a scholarship for a master's degree program. The graduate schools just didn't believe that women needed advanced degrees in science. She also couldn't get a job in her field other than teaching. So she taught and tried her hand at secretarial school and whatever other jobs were deemed acceptable for women in the 1930s, until she landed a position as an unpaid assistant in a lab, which she thought might provide some helpful training. Though she

> "Among immigrant Jews, their one way to success was education, and they wanted all their children to be educated. . . . The person you admired most was the person with the most education."

learned how to use lab equipment, she also endured anti-Semitic jokes from her boss, who eventually started to pay her $20 a week for her labor. She saved up this meager salary and put herself through graduate school, obtaining a master of science degree in chemistry in 1941.

At that point, World War II was underway, and with so many men off fighting in the war, she was able to secure a laboratory job. One of the most accomplished scientists of the 20th century got her start testing the acidity of pickles, monitoring vanilla beans for freshness, and checking the color of the egg yolks used in mayonnaise for a food company.

A second tragedy made Gertrude more eager than ever to get into a lab where she could perform medical research. Her fiancé contracted an infection in his heart. In 1941, the public did not have general access to antibiotics (which were largely reserved for the wartime military), so there was nothing they could do to treat the infection. Six months later, he died of a condition that would have been easily treatable just a few years later in 1945, when penicillin became more available in the US. "It reinforced in my mind the importance of scientific discovery, that it really was a matter of life and death to find treatments for diseases that hadn't been cured before," she said.

In 1946, Gertrude finally got that opportunity when she secured a meeting with George Hitchings at Burroughs, Wellcome & Co., a pharmaceutical business. He believed they could figure out how to trick cancer cells by treating them with artificial compounds that would destroy them but leave normal, healthy cells unharmed. Together they set out to understand the life cycle of diseased cells and what compounds might interrupt their growth. The research was all-consuming, and Gertrude, still determined to continue her formal education, was taking classes at night to earn a PhD. But halfway into her doctoral program, she was told that she had to attend full-time or not at all. Her work was too important at this point—she did not want to walk away from her years of productive research, so she abandoned her pursuit of a doctorate.

With none of the sophisticated tools and technology that today's researchers have, Gertrude and Hitchings developed a deep and novel understanding of the differences between diseased and healthy cells. In 1950, they began testing a drug—a compound called 6MP that Gertrude had developed—on children with leukemia. At that time, a child diagnosed with leukemia had a 40 percent chance of surviving one year. This compound, however, seemed to cure patients, causing

their leukemia to go into remission. Gertrude loved to see patients who were thriving thanks to the drug she had invented. Because it was so promising, the drug was released in 1953, but there was still work to be done. The leukemia came back in many patients—remission was only temporary. There were also negative side effects to the 6MP. Gertrude kept working and released an improved variant called azathioprine in 1957. This drug (in combination with others) today cures childhood leukemia in 80 percent of cases. As important as this development itself was, the method used by Gertrude and Hitchings—focusing on understanding the target of the drug, the diseased cells, rather than simply using trial and error—was a dramatic new approach and led to many other significant discoveries.

In 1962, azathioprine was used in the first successful kidney transplant. Transplants had not been possible before because the body's immune system attacks and rejects an organ that it doesn't recognize as its own. Azathioprine was used to suppress that immune response in organ transplants for the next 20 years.

In 1968, Gertrude began to work on developing an antiviral medication. There was nothing at that time that could kill viruses—many scientists didn't believe it was possible. In 1974, she released the product of her secret research, acyclovir, an antiviral drug that is still used today.

Gertrude retired in 1983, having saved countless lives and changed the field of medical research. In 1984, the team that she had trained was responsible for creating AZT, the only drug available to treat HIV and AIDS at that time. In 1988 she shared the Nobel Prize in Physiology or Medicine with Hitchings and Sir James Black for their role in discovering "Rational drug design" in the development of medications. She also received not one but three honorary PhDs from George Washington University, Brown University, and the University of Michigan, safely making her "the person with the most education."

Ultimately, these accolades weren't as meaningful to her as simply knowing that she'd made a difference. "When you meet someone who has lived for 25 years with a kidney graft, there's your reward."

JUDITH RESNIK

1949–1986

On January 28, 1986, millions of Americans watched as Judith Resnik, in her blue flight suit, smiled, waved, and walked confidently aboard the *Challenger* space shuttle. This was Judith's second trip to space—her confidence was hard-earned. She had already logged just under 145 hours on her first space mission aboard the space shuttle *Discovery* in 1984. During that trip, which was the shuttle's maiden voyage, Judith was filmed floating in the cabin with her all-male crewmates. Her dark, curly Jewish mane hovered above and around her head, forming an eye-catching halo in the zero-gravity environment. (At one point, her hair actually got tangled in the camera she was supposed to be using to photograph Halley's comet!) In the background, her locker was adorned with an "I love Tom Selleck" sticker, and Judith was holding a sign that read "Hi Dad." That was her first mission.

On this second mission, there was another woman on board. Christa McAuliffe was a teacher who won a nationwide contest called the Teacher in Space Project. The program was designed to get kids interested in math, science, and space exploration, and to honor teachers who could then return to their classrooms to share their experience. The first space shuttle—a reusable spacecraft—had launched in 1981. The technology was still relatively new at the time of the 1986 *Challenger* flight, and exciting takeoffs and footage from space were broadcast on TV. This was the first flight with a teacher on board, so it was a very big deal. McAuliffe's students and students around the country were watching the takeoff at 11:38 a.m. And they were all watching when the *Challenger* exploded 73 seconds later, killing everyone on board.

While Judith Resnik may be best known for her tragic death, witnessed by millions of Americans in real time, she also lived a remarkable life during her 36 years on Earth (and in space). She was the first Jewish woman to do a lot of things, most famously, to go into space. But she was outstanding in pretty much whatever she took on, Jewish, female, or not.

Born in Akron, Ohio, to Ukrainian immigrant parents, Judith was smart and STEM-oriented from the get-go, solving challenging math problems before she even started kindergarten. Her father, an optometrist, was also a part-time cantor at Akron's Beth-El synagogue, where Judith was bat mitzvahed. Her mother was a paralegal. Her parents divorced when Judith was 17, and she petitioned the court to live with her father after the divorce.

If she was upset by the divorce, it did not stop her from being both valedictorian and homecoming queen of her high school—and one of only 16 students ever to earn a perfect SAT score. (This was in 1966, a full 40 years after the test was first administered.) Judith had such an abundance of talent that when she graduated from high school, she had to decide if she should become a concert pianist, pursuing her music education at the prestigious Juilliard School in New York City, or whether she would focus on her passion for math and science. She picked STEM over music and decided to go to Carnegie Mellon University, where she received a bachelor's degree in electrical engineering; she later earned a PhD in engineering from the University of Maryland.

While racking up engineering degrees in the 1970s, she worked as an electrical engineer, designing circuit boards, and as a biomedical engineer at the National Institutes of Health. There she performed research on the physiology of vision. Even in a field of exceptionally smart people, Judith rose to the top.

In 1977, the National Aeronautics and Space Administration (NASA) decided to diversify its program, and Nichelle Nichols, the actress who played Lieutenant Uhura on the

"I never play anything softly."

original *Star Trek* TV series, was brought on board to recruit women and people of color to its ranks. It's surprising that it took an actress who played an astronaut from the future on TV to convince a bunch of geniuses to apply to a real-life space program. But that is what happened, and the pitch worked on Judith!

It worked on a lot of people, it turns out. There were 8,000 applicants that year, and NASA accepted 35 of them. On June 28, 1978, Judith Resnik became one of six women in the first astronaut class to include women.

Judith was nearly the first American woman in space—but her classmate Sally Ride edged her out for that honor. She was not the first Jew in space either—Soviet astronaut Boris Volynov was. But she was the first Jewish woman and the first Jewish American to go into space. Her short, incomparable life was packed with firsts.

"I don't want to be a Jewish woman astronaut, I just want to be an astronaut, period. I just want to go out in space and do my job."

Many schools, scholarships, and awards are named in honor of her barrier-breaking bravery. And in the center of the Apollo Basin on the moon, there is a crater that bears her name as well.

JANET YELLEN
1946–

On January 25, 2021, in a hotly divided Senate, on the heels of the most volatile presidential election in at least a century, Janet Yellen was easily confirmed by a vote of 84–15 as the first woman in US history to be named secretary of the Treasury. Thirty-four Republicans had joined all 50 Democratic senators to approve President Biden's choice to lead the country's economy after a year-long pandemic had decimated it. A bunch of senators who couldn't agree on *anything*—almost all agreed that Janet Yellen was their best hope.

Janet grew up in Bay Ridge, Brooklyn, what was then an ethnically mixed neighborhood of Jewish, Scandinavian, Italian, and Irish immigrants. Her parents were nonobservant Polish Jews, both the children of immigrants. They raised Janet and her older brother in an attached two-family home four blocks from the Narrows, a waterway leading to the Hudson River. Her mom was a schoolteacher who had stopped working when she had kids. She managed the family finances and followed the stock market—habits that influenced Janet. Her father was a doctor who had to go to medical school overseas because, starting in the 1920s, American medical schools had quotas limiting the number of Jewish students they would admit. His office was on the ground floor of their brownstone, so Janet would sit on the stoop and see the dockworkers and longshoremen who came to her father. She knew that some of them had lost their jobs and couldn't afford to pay for medical care. And even as a young teenager, she realized that was a huge problem—that the economy did not work for them. Her views about economics were based on this experience and grew out of this neighborhood brimming with hardworking people who couldn't always make ends meet.

She was an extremely gifted student—described by classmates and teachers alike as the smartest person they'd ever met. She attended Fort Hamilton High School, a public school named for the country's first Treasury secretary, Alexander Hamilton. Her family traveled around the world during summer vacations, instilling a love of travel and food—and rocks. Janet was an avid rock collector and spent Saturdays of her junior year in high school taking a geology class and then working on her collection. She was editor in chief of her school newspaper, *The Pilot*, and was class valedictorian. When it was time for the editor to interview the valedictorian, a school tradition, Janet interviewed herself.

After graduating with a slew of awards, she went to Brown University, where her first class in macroeconomics opened her eyes to the kind of impact she could have someday. "I was interested in math, and I think very logically, and I remember sitting in that class and learning about how there were policy decisions that could have been taken during the Great Depression to alleviate all that human suffering—that was a real 'aha' moment for me. I realized that public policy can, and should, address these problems," she recounted years later. She attended a lecture by a Yale professor named James Tobin and was so impressed with him and his theories about how people spent and saved at different stages of life that she went to Yale to

ECONOMICS AT HOME

Janet and her husband practiced one of their own economic theories when they hired their first nanny: they thought it was important to pay more than they needed to, convinced that whoever they hired would do a better job. They believed that large companies could also profit by paying their workers better wages, because they would gain loyalty and more productivity from their employees as a result.

continue her studies in economics with him, earning a PhD in 1971. "Tobin was a person who really impressed me, because he had a passion for social justice and for public policy," she said. She believed in the value of public service and felt that Tobin similarly looked at economic policy as "something that was about making the lives of people better."

She was hired right out of Yale as an assistant professor at Harvard, where she taught for the next six years. She then spent a year working at the Federal Reserve Bank (the "Fed") in Washington, where she met another economist, a man named

George Akerlof, in the cafeteria. They got married that year, in 1977, and had a son who eventually joined the family business, becoming an economist as well. After their year at the Fed, Janet and her husband went back to teaching, first at the London School of Economics and then at the University of California, Berkeley.

But she was drawn to work in government, really as a means of doing good, and in 1994 was nominated to the Federal Reserve Board of Governors by the Clinton administration. Then, in 1997, she chaired Clinton's Council of Economic Advisers, where she studied, among other things, the gender wage gap. She determined that the only reason women were earning less than men was discrimination.

"I come from an intellectual tradition where public policy is important, it can make a positive contribution, it's our social obligation to do this. We can help to make the world a better place."

Whether it's because she was a woman, or Jewish, or just because she was Janet Yellen, she cared deeply about regular working people, and reducing unemployment has been a theme of her career in government. In 2004, she became president of the Federal Reserve Bank of San Francisco, one of 12 regional banks that work with the Fed in Washington, D.C., to determine policy. And then, in 2010, President Obama appointed her as vice chair of the Board of Governors of the Federal Reserve System in Washington, D.C. In 2013, she became the first woman to be named chairman of the Fed. Just a few short years after the financial crisis, she had the most important seat at the most important table in the country. This made her easily one of the most influential women in the world. During this very volatile time at the Fed, unemployment was at its record lowest point—proving her theories about how the government could and should intervene to make life better for people.

In large part due to her record at the Fed, it surprised no one that Janet Yellen was at the top of President Biden's list for Treasury secretary. As the third consecutive Jewish Treasury secretary and the first ever woman to hold that role in the history of the United States, she remains focused on using her science—economics—the way her father used his science: to help real people rebuild their lives after the pandemic. She particularly focuses on fixing things for those hardest hit: women and people of color. In a field based on numbers and dominated by men, Janet took a distinctly female, Jewish approach—making it all about social justice.

FROM HAMILTON TO YELLEN

The secretary of the Treasury is part of the president's cabinet (top advisors)—fifth in the line of succession after the President. The secretary is appointed by the president and confirmed by the Senate. The secretary of the Treasury advises the president on anything having to do with the economy—from budgets to taxes to jobs. The Treasury aims to maintain a strong, stable economy and to create job opportunities. One of Secretary Yellen's first initiatives was to pass a global minimum tax to discourage large corporations from taking their operations to countries with lower tax rates and also to insure that big companies do not avoid paying taxes in their country of origin.

ENTREPRENEURS

ESTÉE LAUDER

1908–2004

Jar of Joy

Josephine Esther Mentzer was born in 1908 to Hungarian Jewish immigrants and raised in a modest house in Corona, Queens—a mostly Italian neighborhood in New York City. Josephine (who went by her middle name, Esther) and her family lived above her father's hardware store, where most of the seven children pitched in at some point. Esther got her first retail and merchandising experience at the unglamorous store on Corona Avenue.

When she was a teenager, her uncle John, a chemist, moved in with the family. He set up a lab in a stable behind the house, where he concocted face creams, explaining to Esther that she shouldn't use harsh detergents to clean her face. She was intrigued and began to help him mix his potions, filling jars with cleansers and moisturizers. She began to take samples to her friends and then would refine the formulas based on their feedback.

Esther loved the beauty business. She introduced what she called "hope in a jar" to local hair salons and began to sell her uncle's creams full-time after she finished high school. When she was 19, she met her husband, Joseph Lauter, a silk merchant who also was the child of Jewish immigrants. They married in 1930, and in 1933 she gave birth to her first son, Leonard.

By then, she started to go by the name Estee, and she was completely driven. By her own admission, Estee focused on work over her family life. She often told about selling her creams in a fancy salon and admiring the blouse a woman there was wearing. She asked the woman where she'd bought her beautiful blouse, and the very condescending woman assured Estee, "You could never afford it." That did not sit well with Estee. She was determined that nobody would ever again talk down to her or make her feel less than. This attitude fed into her insecurity and embarrassment about being the child of immigrants.

Fortunately for her, Estee was a brilliant businesswoman; unfortunately, she couldn't maintain her marriage and her business, and she divorced Joseph in 1939. She moved to Miami and sold her wares to affluent vacationers, reimagining herself as part of that world of money and leisure. But living out what had been her fantasy made her miss her ex-husband, and she and Joseph remarried three years later, becoming business partners as well. She rebranded herself and her business at the same time, adding a glamorous accent to *Estée*,

FAMILY BEAUTY SECRETS

Estée's mother, Rose, who lived until the age of 88, always wore gloves and carried a parasol to guard against the sun's harmful rays. Though Estée appreciated this beauty tip (and had beautiful skin as a result), she was also embarrassed by her mother's parasol and her thick accent.

and the couple changed their last name to Lauder. Estée Lauder also became her brand name, as Estée managed product development and sales and Joseph took over finance and manufacturing. She gave birth to their second son, Ronald, in 1944, and in the 1940s, she expanded the business into upscale department stores like Saks Fifth Avenue and Neiman Marcus. Estée set up her counter and trained the saleswomen herself. She was selling her image—of beauty and success—as much as she was peddling face cream.

In 1953, she launched the product that would take her to the next level. Up until then, perfume was considered an extravagance meant for men to buy for their wives. Estée Lauder's Youth Dew changed all that. It was a bath oil that could be used as perfume, with a reasonable price of $8.50 a bottle, and it was designed for women to purchase for themselves. That first year, 50,000 women did just that. Over the next 30 years, 150 million bottles were sold all around the world.

Beyond her drive and salesmanship, there were a few secrets to Estée's success: She gave out lots of samples and demonstrations so that women could see for themselves the effectiveness of her "jars of hope." And she introduced the idea of "gift with purchase." Every time a customer bought one item, she gave them a sample of something else—expanding the number of products her customers would purchase as well as building loyalty. Before social media was a thing, she encouraged customers to spread the word. "Telephone, telegraph, tell a woman."

The most successful self-made entrepreneur of her generation, Estée was ashamed of her roots, her modest home, and her immigrant parents. She assimilated rather than celebrating her heritage. But once she genuinely became the image of beauty and success that she had always tried to convey, once she could buy any blouse she wanted, when her company was worth well over $200 million (by the early 1980s), she spent the later years of her life embracing "tzedakah" as a generous philanthropist.

> "Measure your success in dollars, not degrees."

DIANE VON FURSTENBERG

1946–

The story of Diane von Furstenberg ends like a fairy tale—complete with a princess, jewels, and beautiful gowns. But her story begins before she was born, with her mother in a terrible place called Auschwitz.

Lily Nahmias was born in Greece and moved to Brussels, Belgium, where she was arrested on May 17, 1944, for being part of the Belgian Resistance (regular people who secretly worked against the Nazis during World War II). At the time, Lily was 20 years old and engaged to Diane's father, Leon Halfin, although he was living in Switzerland. Their romance unfolded in daily love letters. Lily was living in a safe house and spent her days riding her bicycle around Brussels, delivering documents and fake papers to those who needed them. When she was being interrogated after her arrest, she did not give any information about her friends in the Resistance movement. Instead, she declared that she was living in the safe house because she was Jewish. For this more serious crime, she was sent to Auschwitz. Of the 25,631 Belgian Jews who were transported to concentration camps, Lily was one of 1,244 survivors. Weighing just 59 pounds when she was liberated, she survived 13 months in the death camp. Toward the end, when the Nazis knew that the Allies were closing in and tried to force their prisoners into other camps, she survived a weeks-long death march through the snow, although thousands more of the sick and malnourished died as the Nazis shot those who couldn't keep up.

"Fear is not an option."

Lily was miraculously nursed back to health at an American base until she was well enough to travel home to Belgium, where her mother fed her tiny bits of food every 15 minutes for months until she was back to her prewar weight and health. Still, she had been completely transformed on the inside by her experience in the camps. When they reconnected months after the war, Lily barely resembled the sweet, innocent, lighthearted teenager whom Leon had met, fallen in love with, and proposed to by mail. Still, they married and fully disregarded doctors' orders to wait several years before having children. Diane Halfin was born 18 months after their wedding, on New Year's Eve 1946. "I was her victory," Diane has explained.

"My voice catches every time I speak publicly about my mother, and I do in every speech I make, aware that I wouldn't be giving that speech if Lily Nahmias had not been my mother. Sometimes it feels odd that I always bring up her story, but I am compelled to. It explains the child I was, the woman I became."

Leon was a successful businessman, and Diane's childhood was filled with Tintin comic books, private school, seaside vacations, and Belgian pastries. Though the war had cast an unmistakable shadow over their lives—there were days when her mother stayed in bed and

"THIS EXPLAINS WHO I AM."

When Lily was arrested and in a truck on her way to prison, she scribbled a note using a burnt match for a pencil. On one side, she explained what had happened. "I want you to know that I am leaving with a smile, I promise" were the words of comfort she offered to her family. On the back of the note, she wrote her parents' address and a plea to whoever found the note to deliver it. Long after her mother died, Diane's cousin sent an envelope holding the original note to Diane. Although she'd heard stories about this note and her mother's deportation, holding the evidence in her hand shook her. "I am the daughter of someone who went to the concentration camps with a smile," she realized.

didn't speak—the Halfins appeared to be a beautiful, elegant, happy family. Her father showered his curly-haired daughter with love and affection, and her mother taught her strength and fearlessness. When Diane was a little girl and told her mother she was afraid of the dark, her mother locked her in a closet and stood outside of it to show her that there was nothing to be afraid of. "Fear is not an option" was one of the lessons drilled into her by her powerhouse mother. Diane was raised to be fiercely independent—she was sent alone on a train from Brussels to Paris to visit her aunt when she was just nine years old. As a little girl traveling with her parents, Diane was left alone in the hotel room while they went out to dinner. She was sent to boarding school in Lausanne, Switzerland, for two years, and then to another boarding school in Oxford, England. From the start, she loved being on her own, was intensely social, and had tons of glamorous friends and boyfriends.

As she traveled, she learned new languages and relished exploring. She went to the University of Madrid, skied the Alps in the winter, and led a jet-setting life as a teenager. When she was 19 and living in Switzerland, she met Eduard Egon und zu Fürstenberg, an actual Austro-German prince, at a birthday party in Lausanne, Switzerland. Both students at the University of Geneva, they fell in love.

Three years later, in May 1969, after they had both graduated, he surprised her with an enormous sapphire ring and a marriage proposal. She was living in Italy and working for a textile manufacturer, designing silk jersey dresses.

She became pregnant with her first child while celebrating her engagement to Egon. They married that July despite resistance from the Furstenberg side of the family, which was appalled at the idea of their German prince marrying a Jewish woman. His mother's side of the family—heirs to the Fiat automobile fortune, embraced Diane, and his mother even gave them a beach house on the Italian island of Sardinia as a wedding gift! Their son, Alexandre, was born in January 1970 in New York City. Diane gave birth to a daughter, Tatiana, 13 months later. At the same time, she opened the Diane von

Furstenberg Studio and began designing dresses. Despite having two young children under the age of two and working full-time, Prince and Princess von Furstenberg enjoyed a busy, fast, high-profile social life. This soon turned out to be too fast even for Diane. The couple divorced in 1973.

Diane could have kicked back and lived a very nice life, but she did not want alimony from her prince. She wanted to earn her own living. She loved the versatility of the stretchy jersey fabrics she had gotten to know working in Italy. In the background, the women's equal rights movement was in high gear. From that spirit, and the imagination of the princess daughter of a Holocaust survivor, the "wrap dress" was born.

A simple silk jersey dress, it looked good on every body type. Women could slip into and out of it as easily as if it was a bathrobe. It was polished and professional for work, fun and sexy for nights out dancing. It beautifully reflected the women's liberation movement of the '70s, freeing and fashionable. And it caught on! The company was selling 25,000 dresses each week! Diane would definitely not need alimony. Her business empire exploded. Soon, she had a line of cosmetics as well as clothing. She had licensed shoes, purses, sunglasses, and stores all around the world. By the mid-1970s, she had sold millions of dresses, and Diane von Furstenberg was a household name. She launched the fragrance Tatiana in 1975, named for her daughter. She purchased an estate in Connecticut, called Cloudwalk. She had arrived—no prince on a white horse necessary.

But maintaining that level of success had its challenges—there were many twists and turns in both her professional and personal story. In 1978, she sold the original dress license, and then, in 1983, she sold her beauty business as well. "By that time, I had lost control of everything," she recounted. In the 1980s, she stepped back from the fashion business and lived in Bali and then in Paris, where she founded a publishing company.

When she returned to the US in 1990, she launched a home shopping business, Silk Assets. Her very first product had $1.2 million in sales within two hours. She clearly had not lost her magic touch. In the late 1990s, she relaunched her brand and the timeless wrap dress, 25 years after its debut. A whole new market of young women eagerly embraced its simplicity.

In 2001, 26 years after they first met, she married the billionaire entrepreneur Barry Diller. Together, they run the Diller–von Furstenberg Family Foundation, giving millions of dollars each year to causes that are near and dear to them, including the Anti-Defamation League and the Holocaust Museum, many parks and public spaces in New York City, and AIDS research. Diane has pledged to donate half of her fortune to philanthropic efforts.

She continues to work and reimagine her brand and to inspire women around the world with her style, spirit, and strength.

"The most important relationship in your life is the relationship you have with yourself. Because no matter what happens, you will always be with yourself."

In 2018, two sets of sisters appeared on *Forbes* list of the 100 Richest Self-Made Women in the world. One family, the Kardashians, was already well-known. The other set, Susan and Anne Wojcicki, did not star in a reality TV show. Their claim to fame came from growing two different, wildly successful technology companies in Silicon Valley, California.

The Wojcicki sisters' stories begin where every family starts—with their mom.

EMPOWERING

ESTHER WOJCICKI

1941–

Esther Hochman was raised outside of Los Angeles, California, by Russian Jewish parents in a religious Orthodox family. Both of her grandfathers were rabbis. Half of Esther's family had died in the Holocaust, including all of her mother's sisters. Her mother immigrated to the US from Siberia. Her father fled pogroms in the Ukraine. She was the first child on both sides of the family to be born in America.

When Esther was ten years old, her 18-month-old baby brother, David, died after accidentally swallowing a handful of aspirin. Her mother had called the doctor, who advised her to put David to bed. When he became violently ill a few hours later, they took him to four hospitals, all of which refused to treat him because the family was poor. The unnecessary loss of her brother was deeply traumatizing for

Esther and also helped form her approach to life. She realized that her immigrant parents had been afraid to challenge the doctors who first gave them bad advice and then refused to treat their son. Esther grew up determined to speak out, to be unafraid of questioning authority.

She started working as a journalist while a teenager in order to earn money to go to college. Valedictorian of her high school class, she won a scholarship to the University of California, Berkley—becoming the first person in her family to go to college. There, she met Stan Wojcicki, an immigrant Polish Catholic graduate student in physics. They fell in love, and got married, despite both families' displeasure due to their different religious upbringings.

In 1968, Esther Wojcicki became a mom to Susan (followed by Janet and Anne). Stan became a physics professor at Stanford University, and they raised the girls on its campus in Northern California, surrounded by people who valued education above all else. Esther became a teacher when the girls were older, and in 1984 she created the media program at Palo Alto High School. Her successful teaching philosophy, "the Woj Way," was also her parenting philosophy—something she describes as TRICK. The acronym stands for Trust, Respect, Independence, Collaboration, and Kindness.

In her book *How to Raise Successful People*, Esther talks about the importance of trusting children and fostering independence. Her daughters walked to school on their own by the age of five. They also learned responsibility early, earning money by selling lemons picked from a neighbor's tree. And in journalism and life, Esther taught her students and children that it was important to question.

> "I never stepped in their way."

She introduced her daughters to Catholic church and various synagogues, to both Catholic and Jewish holidays. Though Esther was turned off by her strict Orthodox upbringing, one that favored boys over girls, she remained observant, celebrating Shabbat and belonging to synagogue. When each of her daughters reached the age of 12, she allowed them to choose their religion. All three chose Judaism.

SUSAN WOJCICKI

1968–

As a child, Susan was a creative spirit and loved crafting, from candle making to sewing pillows to making spice ropes, which she sold door to door.

After studying literature and history at Harvard University, she earned a master's degree in economics followed by a master's in business administration (MBA). Over the course of her extensive education, the focus of her creative energy shifted to technology. She took a job at Intel, and she and her husband bought a home in Menlo Park, California. In September 1998, when money was tight because of the mortgage and graduate-school loans, they rented out a few bedrooms of their new home to two Stanford students who were starting a business. Larry Page and Sergey Brin used the garage of Susan's home as their office. Over pizza, they talked to Susan about technology and ideas for their business— a search engine they named Google.

In April 2009, pregnant with her first child, Susan became Google's 16th employee. Her job as the first marketing manager was to build a worldwide brand with no budget. She has said, "I wasn't focused on revenue. I was focused on whether this will make a difference in people's lives." This idea of making an impact would be a consistent theme for all of the Wojcickis.

Susan was the company's first mom and responsible for creating its in-house daycare center. She also became a vocal advocate for paid maternity leave, understanding that it was a very effective way of keeping talented women. In addition to being the force behind Google's 18-weeks paid maternity leave policy, she was the brains behind AdSense, Google's revolutionary advertising product. (AdSense is the reason why, if you like purple running shoes, you will see ads for purple running shoes when you are on your favorite website.)

In 2005, a month before YouTube launched, Google had launched its own free video sharing site. In 2006, Susan convinced the founders and the board to buy YouTube, which she felt was doing a better job by sharing crowd-sourced videos. Though it seemed really risky at the time, she believed that it was well worth the $1.65 billion purchase price. Named CEO of YouTube in 2014, she was the company's second CEO and first woman CEO. By 2018, YouTube was valued at $160 billion. Definitely a smart investment.

While she often emphasizes the worldwide community created by YouTube's open platform—such as the woman who started a quilting business that now employs an entire town, or the woman who posted a video diary about living with cystic fibrosis—the size and scope of YouTube's reach created many challenges and scandals too. As CEO, she also had to deal with controversies and difficult decisions about the importance of supporting free speech versus removing hate speech, and the business of keeping users engaged versus allowing the spread and reinforcement of disinformation. It was a delicate balance, and not the only one Susan would have to juggle.

While becoming one of the most powerful women in the tech world, Susan was also raising five children with her husband. Sitting down at the dinner table every night, planning bar mitzvahs, and running a multi-billion-dollar global empire, Susan has been actively living the work-life balance that she advocates for.

"Whether its salary or a promotion or a job, I think it's really important for women to ask for what they think they deserve."

JANET WOJCICKI

1970–

Janet, was born 14 months after Susan. According to Esther, Janet was the most energetic of the three girls as a child and had a gift for languages. After graduating from Gunn High School in Palo Alto, California, she received a bachelor's degree from Stanford, a master's degree in epidemiology, and then a PhD in anthropology. As a Fulbright scholar, she studied breastfeeding in Botswana.

Though less famous than her entrepreneur sisters, Janet is hardly a slouch! An adjunct assistant professor of pediatrics at University of California, San Francisco, she speaks several African dialects and is working to improve the health of children in Swaziland. Her research focuses on childhood obesity, HIV, and maternal and child nutrition. An academic like her parents, Janet's life's work is about making the world a better, healthier place for women.

ANNE WOJCICKI

1973–

Anne, the youngest sister, first heard about DNA and genes when she was five years old and never really stopped thinking about them. But her early dreams focused more on figure skating. Her parents thought she should play tennis rather than skate, but they fully supported her independence. They just weren't going to pay for figure skating lessons. So Anne exchanged babysitting for lessons and became an excellent figure skater before switching over to ice hockey. In high school, she was an editor for the school newspaper, *The Oracle*, and won a scholarship to Yale for her sports stories. There, she played on the women's ice hockey team and earned a biology degree.

She found her way into healthcare investment advising after college but grew disillusioned by Wall Street and quit in 2000. "I started to see this disconnect between what I'm investing in and the people who are actually consuming healthcare," Anne explained. It bothered her that the medical industry was focused on profits— rather than on keeping people healthy.

She planned to go to medical school but she became fascinated by biotech research. The Human Genome Project—a decades-long scientific research project about unraveling the mysteries of human DNA and which genes are connected to which traits, was completed in 2003. Anne wondered, what if there was a dataset for genetic information? In 2006, along with biologists Linda Avey and Paul Cusenza, Anne decided to make her idea a reality and launch a new company called 23andMe. Named after the 23 pairs of chromosomes in a normal human cell, 23andMe's goal was to give the public the ability to have their DNA tested. For a few hundred dollars and a test tube full of spit, regular people would have access to information about their ancestry. If they paid more, they could find out whether they were at risk for certain genetic diseases, such as different types of cancer, Alzheimer's disease, or Parkinson's.

While the tests cost more than the company was charging people, Anne knew the value of the company, and to the world at large, would be in having tons of genetic medical data for scientists. She wanted to empower people with information, believing they could make smarter health decisions if they knew their risks up front. And she hoped to

revolutionize genetic research and drug development. The following year, 23andMe received $8.95 million from many investors, including Anne's then husband, Sergey Brin, who cofounded Google. (The two met through Susan and married in 2007 in a Jewish ceremony under a chuppah in the Bahamas; they divorced in 2015.)

In 2008, 23andMe's DNA testing kit was named invention of the year by *Time* magazine. In 2013, Anne was named Most Daring CEO by *Fast Company*, though the company struggled to get FDA approval. They had to prove that the tests and medical information they were providing directly to people was actually reliable. In 2015, the FDA began to approve their health-related tests. In 2017, Oprah named the $99 ancestry kit one of her "favorite things." In June of 2021, the company was valued at more than $3 billion, making Anne's shares worth over $1 billion. As Anne had imagined, a genetic database was extremely valuable.

> "My parents rarely said no to anything. They gave me incredible decision-making power and helped guide those decisions."

Each of the Wojcicki sisters figured out how to have an impact in her own way, embracing the idea of *tikkun olam* ("repairing the world") on a gigantic scale. All of the sisters live within driving distance of their parents and one another, and they frequently get together with their gaggle of children. In many ways, they're just like other close-knit Jewish families. They just happen to be worth billions of dollars.

LESS GOLDA MEIR UNBREAKABLE HANNAH SENESH TRAILBLAZING BELLA A
OUS SIMONE VEIL TIRELESS DIANNE FEINSTEIN FEARLESS GOLDA MEIR UNB
SENESH TRAILBLAZING BELLA ABZUG COURAGEOUS SIMONE VEIL TIRELES
FEARLESS GOLDA MEIR UNBREAKABLE HANNAH SENESH TRAILBLAZING BEL
OUS SIMONE VEIL TIRELESS DIANNE FEINSTEIN FEARLESS GOLDA MEIR UNB
SENESH TRAILBLAZING BELLA ABZUG COURAGEOUS SIMONE VEIL TIRELES
FEARLESS GOLDA MEIR UNBREAKABLE HANNAH SENESH TRAILBLAZING BEL
OUS SIMONE VEIL TIRELESS DIANNE FEINSTEIN FEARLESS GOLDA MEIR UNB
SENESH TRAILBLAZING BELLA ABZUG COURAGEOUS SIMONE VEIL TIRELES
FEARLESS GOLDA MEIR UNBREAKABLE HANNAH SENESH TRAILBLAZING BEL
OUS SIMONE VEIL TIRELESS DIANNE FEINSTEIN FEARLESS GOLDA MEIR UNB
SENESH TRAILBLAZING BELLA ABZUG COURAGEOUS SIMONE VEIL TIRELES
FEARLESS GOLDA MEIR UNBREAKABLE HANNAH SENESH TRAILBLAZING BEL
OUS SIMONE VEIL TIRELESS DIANNE FEINSTEIN FEARLESS GOLDA MEIR UNB
SENESH TRAILBLAZING BELLA ABZUG COURAGEOUS SIMONE VEIL TIRELES
FEARLESS GOLDA MEIR UNBREAKABLE HANNAH SENESH TRAILBLAZING BEL
OUS S **LEADERS** SS DIANNE FEINSTEIN FEARLESS GOLDA MEIR UNB
SENE ELLA ABZUG COURAGEOUS SIMONE VEIL TIRELES
FEARLESS GOLDA MEIR UNBREAKABLE HANNAH SENESH TRAILBLAZING BEL
OUS SIMONE VEIL TIRELESS DIANNE FEINSTEIN FEARLESS GOLDA MEIR UNB

GOLDA MEIR

1898–1978

n 1969, Golda Meir became only the third woman to lead a country in the 20th century. Sixty-five years earlier, as a little girl in Ukraine, she hid from the violent, anti-Semitic Cossacks. The fear she felt—and a yearning to never feel vulnerable as a Jew—drove Golda from the beginning to the end of her life.

Goldie Mabovitch was born in Kiev, Ukraine, one of eight children, only three of whom survived to adulthood. When she grew up in the 1890s and early 1900s, anti-Semitism was so intense in most of Russia and Ukraine that it was impossible for Jews to live there safely or comfortably. Golda's father, a carpenter, couldn't get work or wouldn't be paid for work he completed. Later in life, Golda would describe the constant fear of pogroms. She recalled the sound of her father and a Jewish neighbor boarding up their doors and windows. The family had no money, little to eat, and no reason to hope things would change. So in 1903, her father emigrated to the United States in search of a better life. In many families, the fathers and older sons would emigrate first and earn enough money to then send for the others.

Golda's mother, Bluma, took Golda, her older sister Sheyna, and their baby sister Tzipka to live with her family in Pinsk (now part of Belarus). Pinsk was a muddy little shtetl (a Jewish village) built alongside a river. Bluma's sisters and their children were also crammed into her parents' house during this difficult time. Shortly after they moved, a few hundred miles away in a town called Kishinev, there was a massacre so violent and bloody that it became a turning point for many Russian Jews. Stunned by the intensity of this pogrom, which raged for days and left 50 dead and 500 wounded and destroyed thousands of homes, Jews all over the Russian Empire held a day of fasting in sympathy. Even though she was only five years old at the time, Golda insisted on fasting too.

In America, Golda's father had found work on the railroad in Milwaukee, Wisconsin, and saved enough money to send for the family. So in the spring of 1906, Golda, her mother, and two sisters took a daunting six-week journey—packing onto trains from Russia to Poland to Belgium, where they set sail for Quebec, Canada, and then boarded another train for Milwaukee. Their bags were stolen along the way, and they arrived with $12, the soiled clothes on their backs, and "fear, hunger, and fear," as Golda would later describe it.

POGROMS

Pogroms were violent attacks on homes and businesses in Jewish neighborhoods. There were two major waves of pogroms, and they took place primarily in Russia, Poland, Ukraine, and Belarus in the 1880s and then again from 1917 to 1920. (Though the years in between were not exactly peaceful.) Sometimes police and soldiers participated in these mob attacks, where Jews were injured and killed, property was destroyed, and homes were looted. Between 1900 and 1920, more than 2 million Jews emigrated to the United States to escape anti-Semitic violence.

Their father outfitted the girls in American department store dresses, and the family settled into their new, safe life in the Jewish quarter of this Midwestern city. There were six synagogues, Jewish-run delis and shops, schools, clubs, and services for refugees funded and run by Jews who had arrived earlier. Everyone in the community spoke Yiddish and went to English language classes. Bluma opened a grocery store that, over time, expanded into a successful deli.

By the time Golda was ten years old, she had become an activist, organizing a small group of students to raise funds for textbooks for students who couldn't afford them. Even though she was often late to school because she had to help out in her mother's store, Golda graduated at the top of her class and was eager to go to high school and then become a teacher. Her parents wanted her to go to secretarial school and get an office job, so Golda ran away to live with Sheyna, who had moved to Denver, Colorado, and married. Sheyna was also very political and involved with other socialist Zionists who would meet in their home. (Zionists believed in creating a Jewish homeland in what was then Palestine.) It was at these meetings that Golda first started to hear about kibbutzim in Palestine, Jewish farming settlements. She realized that, although in the US people were *talking about* these ideals of communal living and sharing and equality, in Palestine the Jewish settlers were making it happen. She met her future husband, Morris Myerson, at one of these Zionist meetings. Golda's dream of moving to a kibbutz in Palestine quickly overtook her dream of becoming a teacher. In 1915, she joined Workers of Zion, a Zionist organization that became the center of her social life and her activism.

WHAT IS A KIBBUTZ?

Kibbutzim are communal farms where Jewish settlers live and work. The first kibbutz was formed in 1907 by Mania Shochat in what was then Palestine. The idea is that everyone contributes something—planting, picking, building, cooking, teaching, childcare—and all of the kibbutzniks' needs are taken care of by others in the community.

When she married Morris in 1917, she let him know that they would be moving to Palestine. She was not open to negotiation on this point. That year, the Balfour Declaration was issued, and the dream of every Zionist suddenly seemed within reach. A letter written by the British foreign secretary Arthur Balfour and addressed to Lionel Rothschild, a powerful British Jew, stated that Britain intended to establish a "national home for the Jewish people" in Palestine.

Her dream in her sights, Golda Myerson rose through the ranks of Workers of Zion, protested, raised money for Zionist causes, and worked multiple jobs to save money for their move. Four years later, she and Morris boarded a ship along with Sheyna and her daughter and Golda's closest girlhood friend, Regina. She arrived in Tel Aviv in 1921 and joined Kibbutz Merhavia. There, Golda threw herself into picking almonds, baking bread, and caring for chickens. She was so productive that after one year, she was elected to the kibbutz's three-person steering committee—her first elected position.

Golda and Morris left the kibbutz after three years and had a son, Menahem, and then a daughter, Sara. They moved to Tel Aviv and then to Jerusalem, and Golda became more and more involved in politics and activism, eventually taking on a senior role with the Women Workers' Council. For this job, she moved back to Tel Aviv, away from Morris, effectively ending their marriage. Her children were still young and living with her, and she was extremely conflicted about working and traveling so much. She went to conferences in Europe to meet with other socialist leaders. She took fundraising trips to the United States. Since she traveled by trains and boats, she would be gone for months at a time. But with so much that needed to be done for Jews in Palestine, she couldn't not work.

As Nazism expanded in Germany and Austria in the 1930s, tens of thousands of Jews from those countries began pouring into Palestine each year—with well over 100,000 arriving between 1933 and 1935. In 1938, Golda attended a conference of 32 nations, organized by US president Franklin Roosevelt, with the goal of figuring out how to handle the refugee crisis. Nobody opened their doors to the hundreds of thousands of Jews being driven from their homes in Germany and Austria. Only the Dominican Republic offered to settle 100,000 refugees. Golda realized that a Jewish homeland was the only place that Jews would be safe, and it was more important than ever to help them get to Palestine.

In 1939, as Hitler was about to launch World War II by invading Poland, Britain decided to limit Jewish immigration to Palestine as well. Jews had nowhere to go to escape slaughter in Europe! Golda was now a leader with Histadrut, a political organization, and part of her job was to communicate and negotiate with the British government. She knew that the only way to deal with them at this critical moment in time was to disobey them. She worked closely with Haganah, the secret Jewish defense force, to help smuggle in Jewish refugees by boat. Tens of thousands of unauthorized immigrants were brought in illegally because they would have died otherwise. Golda raised millions of dollars

> "To me, being Jewish means and has always meant being proud to be part of a people that has maintained its distinct identity for more than 2,000 years, with all the pain and torment that has been inflicted upon it."

from American Jews to help bring European Jews to Palestine and also to build, grow, and defend Jewish settlements. It was crucial to ensure that Jews would have a safe place to go and to stay. As she explained when she met with wealthy Americans, "There is no other Zionism now except for the rescue of Jews."

During World War II, when Palestine was still under British control and European Jews were being rounded up, sent to concentration camps, and mass murdered, the Jews in Palestine were not sure how to secure the future of a Jewish homeland. Golda was thoroughly frustrated, reasoning, "Britain is trying to prevent the growth and expansion of the Jewish community in Palestine, but it should remember the Jews were here 2,000 years before the British came."

On May 8, 1945, when Germany surrendered, Golda could not celebrate. As early as 1943, she had lobbied the United States to bomb Auschwitz, to destroy the gas chambers and roads and railway lines to prevent the slaughter they knew was taking place. But the US didn't listen. Golda and Jews all around the world were devastated as details of the atrocities were confirmed: 6 million Jews dead. The enormity of the loss was too much to absorb.

There were also hundreds of thousands of survivors—refugees with nowhere to go. Most of them did not want to return to their home countries, to the neighbors who had stood by while they were rounded up, who looted their homes while they were in concentration camps. Britain was dragging its feet about allowing refugees into Palestine. The US was still strictly limiting the number of Jews it would allow to immigrate. And the fate of a Jewish state was still up in the air.

Finally, the United Nations agreed that Palestine would be released from British control and divided between Jews and Arab Palestinians. Golda was among the small group of 37 leaders, the Provisional Council of State, organizing to prepare Israel for statehood. Golda was sent on a secret mission to meet with Jordan's King Abdullah in an effort to win a promise from him that Jordan would not attack Israel. He could not make that promise. In anticipation of what would become a five-front war the minute the British pulled out of Palestine, Golda went to the US to raise money for weapons, tanks, and an air force. Wealthy American Jews were their only hope, and Golda knew how to connect with them. She told stories of the bold Jewish pioneers in Palestine who were farming the land and building roads and cities, who needed to defend the only land where Jews could feel safe and welcome. In two weeks of meeting with groups of philanthropists, she raised what was then the astonishing sum of $50 million.

On the afternoon of May 14, 1948, Golda Myerson, along with the other provisional council members, signed Israel's declaration of independence. In comments directed toward Palestinian Arabs after

UNBREAKABLE HANNAH SENESH

As part of an effort to support the Allies during World War II, Golda and other Jewish leaders in Palestine had been pushing the British Royal Air Force (RAF) to let them drop a Jewish force behind enemy lines by parachute. They believed that their volunteers could establish contact with resistance units to fight the Nazis. They also wanted to give hope to Jewish survivors and let them know that Palestine would welcome them after the war. Finally in 1944, the RAF agreed to help 32 Jewish parachutists drop into Italy, Austria, and some other eastern European countries after intensive training.

The 20 who survived the mission found resistance fighters or fought alongside Allied forces. One managed to rescue hundreds of Romanian orphans and send them to Palestine. Some connected with Zionist youth groups.

Hannah Senesh, a 23-year-old poet, was one of three women in the group. When she was dropped into Hungary, it was the first time she'd returned since she left for Palestine five years earlier. She was one of 12 from the original group who were captured. She was tortured but wouldn't provide any information. Her mother was arrested and was shocked to see her daughter not only in Hungary but also bruised, beaten, and with broken teeth. Still, Hannah wouldn't break. Found guilty of spying, she was given the choice of begging for a pardon or facing death by firing squad. She would not beg, and she would not wear a blindfold. Instead, she stared down her murderers.

Hannah's mother was released, survived the war, and emigrated to Palestine, where she reunited with Hannah's brother and published Hannah's poetry.

the signing, she said, "You have fought your battle against us in the United Nations. The partition plan is a compromise; not what you wanted, not what we wanted. But now let us live in peace together."
On May 15, as expected, Egypt attacked Israel from the south. Syria and Lebanon attacked from the north, and Iraq from the east. King Abdullah's Jordanian army captured Jerusalem, holding Jews prisoner. Golda went back to the US to raise more money for arms, for immigrants, and also for the Arab villages in Israel. Israel survived its first war.

In 1949 David Ben-Gurion was elected first prime minister of Israel and was determined to have Golda in his cabinet. She became minister of Labor and Social Insurance. It was her job to create housing and jobs for the hundreds of thousands of Jews immigrating to Israel from Europe and Arab countries. The population more than doubled in Israel's first four years of statehood, but Golda and the rest of the government leaders insisted that any Jew who wanted to immigrate to Israel should be welcomed. This monumental task could not be done easily or well. She had to institute unpopular taxes on people who were barely earning a living in order to feed and shelter people who had absolutely nothing. She had to choose between building a lot of cheap, small homes or fewer better ones, or doing whatever was necessary so that the unprecedented number of refugees would have some kind of shelter, something to eat. She loved the challenge.

In 1956, Ben-Gurion made her foreign minister, officially representing Israel in dealing with leaders around the world. (She was asked to take an Israeli name for this role, as a symbolic gesture, so she started going by Golda Meir, rather than Myerson, at this time.) She developed a close relationship with the United States and Latin American countries. She also created ties with newly independent African countries, including Ghana and Nigeria. And at home, she helped to unite three political parties to create one more powerful Labor party.

She had lived an extraordinary life and was ready to retire in 1966. Her health wasn't good—she had always suffered from migraines and gall bladder issues and was being treated for lymphoma. But the newly united Labor party wasn't quite ready to let her go. In 1969, Prime Minister Levi Eshkol died of a heart attack while in office. Golda was recruited to take his spot.

In a long, difficult life, one of her biggest challenges lay ahead. On Yom Kippur, October 6, 1973, Egypt and Syria launched a surprise attack on Israel, and Israel was caught completely off guard. Intelligence reports had been conflicting, and Golda's military advisors did not think there was an imminent threat. Not quite convinced that things would be quiet, she had called up the reserves—most of Israel's army was not active duty—but they were not yet in place. It was a costly and frightening war for Israel. Eventually, with weapons support from the US, Israel regained its territory and security and negotiated a peace agreement with Egypt. But Golda would never forgive herself for the 2,400 soldiers' lives lost. She described the dramatic way the Yom Kippur War changed her: "I smile, I laugh, I listen to music. But in my heart, it is not the same Golda."

She would be reelected, but there was a lot of anger toward her cabinet, particularly her secretary of defense, Moshe Dayan. So Golda resigned. She continued to represent Israel and to unify Jews around the world in her lifelong mission of supporting a Jewish homeland until the day she died.

"There is only one thing I hope to see before I die and that is that my people should not need expressions of sympathy anymore."

BELLA ABZUG
1920–1998

Bella Savitsky was born in the Bronx, New York, a month before women won the right to vote in 1920. Her parents were very religious Russian immigrants who belonged to an Orthodox synagogue and sent Bella to the Talmud Torah school. She was such a strong student that she was recruited by her teacher to join a Zionist group. The other student members became her close circle of friends. Together they learned, played, and raised money for the Jewish homeland in their Jewish neighborhood, with Bella giving passionate speeches at subway stops.

Bella's father, Emmanuel, was a pacifist who opposed World War I and named his Manhattan butcher shop the Live and Let Live Meat Market to signify his views. When Bella was just 13, he died. The meat market had gone out of business by then, so Bella's mother, Esther, supported the family by working in local department stores. Though it's traditional for sons to recite the Mourner's Kaddish every day for 11 months after a parent dies, Bella didn't have any brothers, so she took on the ritual. Every day before school, she would show up at synagogue and pray. The rabbi and male congregants were not welcoming to a girl. As she recalled, "I stood apart in the corner. The men scowled at me, but no one stopped me. It was those mornings that taught me you could do unconventional things."

Emboldened, she continued to challenge conventions. Bella went to Hunter College, which was then a tuition-free New York City school. While serving as student council president, she led demonstrations against Nazism and the harm being done to Jews in Europe. She also lobbied to add classes in African American and Jewish history. On

"This woman's place is in the house . . . the House of Representatives!"

the weekends, she tutored Hebrew and Jewish history. She earned a scholarship to Columbia Law School, where she was one of just seven women in a class of 120—though she interrupted her studies for a few years to work in a shipbuilding factory during World War II.

When she graduated in 1945, she joined a progressive law firm where she went to work on behalf of labor unions and tenants' and civil rights. On the heels of the Holocaust, she was determined to help poor people and minorities gain justice.

When Martin Abzug, a writer she dated during law school, proposed marriage to Bella, she accepted on the condition that she would continue to work. Not only did he agree, but he supported her career by typing all of her briefs for her. (Bella refused to learn to type because she was concerned that the men in her law firm would ask her to type for them.)

Bella and Martin had two daughters, in 1949 and 1952, and Bella opened her own law office. The family moved from an integrated suburb north of New York City to Greenwich Village. In 1961, along with some college friends, she created Women Strike for Peace. The group lobbied for a nuclear test ban treaty and later protested the war in Vietnam. Community organizing was a second job for Bella, another way for her to promote peace, civil rights, and women's equality.

In 1970, at the age of 50, Bella decided it was time to make change from within, rather than protesting the system. She ran for a congressional seat in her district in New York City. Her feminist slogan? "This woman's place is in the house . . . the House of Representatives." She became the second Jewish woman to serve in Congress.

WHO'S THAT LADY IN THE HAT?

Early in her career when she was working as a labor lawyer representing unions, Bella realized that she was often overlooked when she entered an office. So she started to wear hats to get noticed. A stylish hat became her signature look.

On her first day in office, Bella introduced legislation demanding the withdrawal of US forces from Vietnam. It did not pass, but it quickly established her as a fearless voice of change. She cast her first vote to pass the Equal Rights Amendment. During her first term, she coauthored the Child Development Act with Brooklyn congresswoman Shirley Chisholm (who was the first Black congresswoman, first Black presidential candidate, and an outspoken feminist as well). As she explained to her colleagues on the House floor, "Without adequate, low-cost day care facilities, women are doomed to occupy low-paying, low-prestige jobs." Abzug also introduced groundbreaking legislation aimed at increasing the rights of lesbians and gays. The bill called for amending the Civil Rights Act of 1964 "to prohibit discrimination on the basis of sexual or affectional preference." This was the first bill ever to address gay rights. Her work also led to banning discrimination against women in obtaining credit, loans, and mortgages. She was extremely progressive—somewhat like an Alexandria Ocasio-Cortez of the 1970s.

In 1976, in lieu of seeking a third term, she decided to run for the Senate. It really bothered her that there was not a single woman in the Senate at that time, in spite of the fact that women made up 51 percent of the US population. She narrowly lost the election, and the following year, lost a run for mayor of New York City as well. The climate had become more conservative. Though she failed to win elective office again, she remained active in the feminist movement, regularly addressing international women's conferences. In 1977, she presided over the first National Women's Conference in Houston, where female

ALSO TO HER CREDIT. . .

Now it seems crazy that even though Bella ran her own law firm, she could not get a credit card without her husband's signature until passage of the Equal Credit Opportunity Act of 1974. The law, which she introduced, made it illegal for companies to refuse credit on the basis of gender, race, religion, and national origin.

delegates from all over the country voted on a women's platform. In 1990, she cofounded the Women's Environment and Development Organization (WEDO), an international activist and advocacy network. As WEDO president, Bella became an influential leader at the United Nations and UN world conferences, working to empower women all around the globe.

She was way ahead of the curve in terms of getting people to think about women's issues as they relate to climate change. In her final public speech at the UN Commission on the Status of Women before she died in 1998, she also summarized her life's purpose: "We cannot be free as long as our human rights are violated, as long as we don't have economic equality, and as long as we are not participating in gender-balanced political bodies."

"I've always believed women will change the nature of power rather than power will change the nature of women."

SIMONE VEIL
1927–2017

Simone Jacobs was the youngest of four siblings born in Nice, France, to André, an award-winning architect, and Yvonne. The family was not religious, they were assimilated.

But religious observance did not matter to the Nazis. Jews were Jews. After the Nazis invaded France in 1940, Jews were ordered to register their families, creating what became known as the "Jewish file." At first, Jews were punished with harsh anti-Semitic laws. Their businesses were closed and their property was seized. Later, the French and German police rounded up and deported Jews.

In March 1944, when Simone was just 16, she was arrested by German soldiers. The rest of her family was rounded up over the next weeks. Simone, her mother, and her oldest sister, Madeline were deported to Auschwitz, a concentration camp in Poland, after a harrowing three-day journey in a crowded cattle cart. André and Simone's brother were sent to a different camp in Lithuania. They were never seen again. Simone's sister Denise had joined the French Resistance in Lyon. (The Resistance consisted of volunteer spies and fighters who secretly banded together to work against the Nazis and their French collaborators.) Denise was arrested a few months later, treated as an enemy soldier, and sent to a different prison camp.

When Simone arrived at Auschwitz, she lied about her age because she was warned that most young people were sent straight to the gas chamber. Along with the other prisoners, she was shaved and tattooed and put to work. She became inmate number 78651. As she described in her memoir, *A Life*, "Each of us was just a number, seared into our flesh . . . a number we had to learn by heart since we had lost all identity."

Until January of the next year, Simone, Madeleine, and their mother dug trenches, moved boulders, and fought to stay alive every single day. As the Allies were approaching Auschwitz, the camp was evacuated. Emaciated, beaten down, and exhausted, the women were forced to move to German territory as part of the infamous death marches. The Nazis were trying to hide evidence of the camps and also to hold on to their prisoners for as long as possible. They were sent to Bergen-Belsen, a concentration camp in Germany. There Simone worked in the kitchen. Her mother died in the same typhus epidemic there that killed Anne Frank, also shortly before the end of the war.

On April 15, 1945, Allied troops liberated Bergen-Belsen. Simone and her sister Madeleine had survived. Barely. When a British officer asked Simone how old she was, he thought the war-ravaged 17-year-old must be in her 40s. Denise also survived torture and imprisonment at Ravensbrück, a concentration camp in Germany.

Simone had passed her baccalaureate exam—the equivalent of graduating from high school with honors—just weeks prior to her capture. After the war, she returned to France determined to continue her education. She studied law at the University of Paris and Institut d'Études Politiques, where she met Antoine Veil. She married him in October 1946, and they had three sons. There was some happiness, but also more tragedy. Madeleine, who had survived the concentration camps alongside Simone and became a surrogate mother afterward, died in a car accident seven years later. Simone and her surviving sister, Denise, were once again devastated by loss.

Simone's father André had insisted that her mother quit her studies in chemistry after they were married. This act of sexism drove Simone to do the exact opposite and to spend her professional life fighting for women's rights. Simone became a lawyer in 1956 and was determined to use her position to improve life for prisoners and for women. In her first official role, she worked in the Ministry of Justice and focused on prison reform, wanting to insure that nobody suffered the inhumane treatment that she had endured. A fierce feminist, she also worked to make contraception (birth control pills) widely available.

In 1973, she pushed through laws to make birth control pills both legal and reimbursable (which would make them accessible to all).

She is most famous for her work as the minister of health, a role she took on in 1974. On November 26 of that year, 22 months after the *Roe v. Wade* decision made abortion legal in the US, Simone addressed the National Assembly in France. She explained to the hundreds of male lawmakers, "No woman resorts to an abortion with a light heart. One only has to listen to them: it is always a tragedy.... We can no longer shut our eyes to the 300,000 abortions that each year mutilate

> "I'm often asked what gave me the strength and will to continue the fight. I believe deeply that it was my mother; she has never stopped being present to me, next to me."

the women of this country, trample on its laws and humiliate or traumatize those who undergo them." She was so persuasive that when the law passed, it became Loi Veil, the "Veil law." Thanks to Simone, French women gained the right to terminate a pregnancy.

Her next focus became the unification of Europe. Having seen the trauma and destruction of countries turning against one another, she felt that a strong European union was the only assurance against large-scale conflict. In 1979, French President Jacques Chirac nominated her to represent France in the European Parliament, and then she was elected president of that body. The first woman to hold that position, she held it for three terms through 1982.

During those years, Simone was one of the most powerful women in Europe. She was also controversial—for her feminist views, for her desire to bring Europeans of all different backgrounds together, and for her religion. Anti-Semitism hardly disappeared after the Holocaust. She was often attacked by France's Far Right party, the National Front. But that didn't stop her. She could not be intimidated. She told her opponents, "You do not frighten me. I have survived worse than you!"

L'ACADÉMIE FRANÇAISE

In 2008, Simone became one of only four women (of 700 total members) to be elected to the Académie Française in over 370 years. Founded in 1635, this elite group of writers, scientists, and politicians is charged with maintaining the integrity of the French language. It is an old and revered cultural institution. Each member is given a ceremonial sword. Three things were engraved on Simone's: her Auschwitz tattoo number, 78651; the motto of the French Republic, "Liberty Equality, Fraternity"; and the European Union motto, "United in Diversity."

DIANNE FEINSTEIN

1933 –

Dianne Goldman was born in San Francisco to Leon, a surgeon, and Betty, a former model. Her father's side of the family were observant Jews. Leon's father founded several synagogues in California. Her mother's family, the Rosenburgs, came from St. Petersburg in Russia. Originally Jewish, they began to identify as Russian Orthodox Christians in the late 19th century. During this period, many Jews, Muslims, and other non-Christians living in Russia either converted or claimed to be Russian Orthodox in order to avoid discrimination.

Dianne's mother was abusive with a violent, volatile temper that terrified Dianne and her two younger sisters. Dianne was close with her paternal uncle Morris, who worked as a clothing manufacturer in the garment district and opened her eyes to the working class. He also took her to San Francisco's City Hall to watch a meeting of the Board of Supervisors—her introduction to city politics.

Dianne was the first non-Catholic to attend the Convent of the Sacred Heart High School. She was sent there because her teachers felt that she needed more discipline. By her senior year, she was voted class president—winning her first election. She also went to Hebrew school, where she was confirmed. Though not observant, she told *Mother Jones*, "I am religious in my thinking." At Stanford University, she discovered a love of politics: there she won her second election for class vice president and formed the campus's first Young Democrats club.

> "Women have begun to see that if I go through that doorway, I take everybody through it."

In 1956, Dianne married a lawyer and had a baby, Katherine. But her marriage ended after three years in large part because her husband did not believe that women should work. Not long after she became a divorced single mother, Dianne began one of the longest, most successful political careers in history. Her first appointment came in 1960 when Governor Edmund S. Brown asked her to join the California Women's Board of Terms and Paroles, where she served from 1960 to 1966. This job shaped her views about the criminal justice system.

In 1969, Dianne's career of "firsts" began in earnest. She was the first woman elected to head the Board of Supervisors. During her eighth year in this office, tragedy struck San Francisco: Mayor George Moscone and Board Supervisor Harvey Milk, Dianne's colleagues, were assassinated down the hall from her. She was then appointed the first female mayor to finish the term. She did such a good job helping heal the city that she was easily elected for the maximum two terms. After an unsuccessful bid for governor in 1992, she ran to fill the Senate seat vacated by her opponent. She won, becoming the first Jewish woman in the Senate. In 2009, she became the first woman to chair the Select Committee on Intelligence. Feinstein also became the first woman to serve in the role of top Democrat on the Senate Judiciary Committee in 2017.

During her three decades in the Senate, she became well-known and well-liked for being able to work with Republicans and to get things done. She passed a landmark ten-year assault weapons ban in 1994. She worked to protect immigrants, women, and children—and vowed to continue doing so as long as she could. And she did unpopular things too—including investigating and then publishing a report on the CIA's use of torture in 2014.

Though she won her 2012 election with more votes than any Senate candidate ever up to that point, in 2018, at the age of 85, many people were surprised to see her running for a sixth term. But the workaholic who was known to drag big binders of reading material home from the office every night just didn't think her work was done. She felt compelled to serve until she couldn't.

"Let the record show that you can be a United States senator for 21 years. You can be 79 years old. You can be the chair of the Senate Select Committee on Intelligence, and one of the most recognizable and widely respected veteran public servants in your nation. But if you are female while all of those things, men who you defeat in arguments will still respond to you by calling you hysterical and telling you to calm down."

BARBARA BOXER

When Barbara Boxer was elected to the US Senate shortly after Dianne Feinstein, the two became the first pair of women to represent a state (California) in the Senate. They were also the first two Jewish women in the Senate. She served for 24 years with a focus on the environment and women's rights.

NOTORIOUS RUTH BADER GINSBURG BRILLIANT ELENA KAGAN NOTORIOUS R
NSBURG BRILLIANT ELENA KAGAN NOTORIOUS RUTH BADER GINSBURG BRIL
AN NOTORIOUS RUTH BADER GINSBURG BRILLIANT ELENA KAGAN NOTORIOU
NSBURG BRILLIANT ELENA KAGAN NOTORIOUS RUTH BADER GINSBURG BRIL
AN NOTORIOUS RUTH BADER GINSBURG BRILLIANT ELENA KAGAN NOTORIOU
NSBURG BRILLIANT ELENA KAGAN NOTORIOUS RUTH BADER GINSBURG BRIL
AN NOTORIOUS RUTH BADER GINSBURG BRILLIANT ELENA KAGAN NOTORIOU
NSBURG BRILLIANT ELENA KAGAN NOTORIOUS RUTH BADER GINSBURG BRIL
AN NOTORIOUS RUTH BADER GINSBURG BRILLIANT ELENA KAGAN NOTORIOU
NSBURG BRILLIANT ELENA KAGAN NOTORIOUS RUTH BADER GINSBURG BRIL
AN NOTORIOUS RUTH BADER GINSBURG BRILLIANT ELENA KAGAN NOTORIOU
NSBURG BRILLIANT ELENA KAGAN NOTORIOUS RUTH BADER GINSBURG BRIL
AN NOTORIOUS RUTH BADER GINSBURG BRILLIANT ELENA KAGAN NOTORIOU
NSBURG BRILLIANT ELENA KAGAN NOTORIOUS RUTH BADER GINSBURG BRIL
AN NOTORIOUS RUTH BADER GINSBURG BRILLIANT ELENA KAGAN NOTORIOU
NSBU

JUSTICES

AN N(GINSBURG BRILLIANT ELENA KAGAN NOTORIOU
BURG BRILLIANT ELENA KAGAN NOTORIOUS RUTH BADER GINSBURG BRILLIAN
RIOUS RUTH BADER GINSBURG BRILLIANT ELENA KAGAN NOTORIOUS RUTH
BRILLIANT ELENA KAGAN NOTORIOUS RUTH BADER GINSBURG BRILLIANT

NOTORIOUS

RUTH BADER GINSBURG

1933–2020

Before she was known as the iconic Notorious RBG, before she became an action figure and a bobblehead, before her face—framed by oversized black glasses and a white lace collar—graced T-shirts and tote bags, Joan Ruth Bader was a really smart Jewish girl from Brooklyn. (She went by her middle name because there were too many Joans in her school.) Her mother, Celia, raised Ruth with a deep understanding of the importance of *tikkun olam* ("repairing the earth"). Ruth grew up in the shadow of the Holocaust, a time when the drive to heal was particularly urgent. At 13 years of age, she contributed an essay to her synagogue's newsletter that reflected on the need to defeat prejudice. In it, she wrote, "The war has left a bloody trail and many deep wounds not too easily healed. . . . We are part of a world whose unity has been almost completely shattered. No one can feel free from danger and destruction until the many torn threads of civilization are bound together again."

> "Fight for the things that you care about, but do it in a way that will lead others to join you."

Glimmers of the woman who would make justice her job could be seen not only in the wisdom and maturity of her essay but also in her anger over the fact that boys had bar mitzvahs at 13 while there were no comparable rituals to mark a girl's adulthood. Her passions for gender equality and social justice took shape at an early age.

Ruth's father, Nathan, was a Russian immigrant. As a Jew, he was not allowed to get an education in Russia. Ruth's mother had worked in a garment factory to help pay for her brother's college education, sacrificing her own. Nathan and Celia raised Ruth to value her own education, and she excelled at James Madison High School in their working-class neighborhood in Brooklyn. After battling cancer, Celia died the day before Ruth's graduation.

Ruth left Brooklyn for Cornell University and graduated first in her class with a degree in government in 1954. She married Martin Ginsburg, a charming and outgoing law student, later that year. Ruth described him as "the only young man I dated who cared that I had a brain." She became pregnant that same year, and Martin, who was in the Reserve Officers' Training Corp (ROTC) was called to serve in Oklahoma a few months before their daughter, Jane, was born. Ruth took care of the baby while Martin served.

When she was accepted to Harvard Law School, one of nine women in a class of more than 500—she made the decision to find a way to juggle her studies and childcare. And she faced challenges beyond caring for a one-year-old while studying at one of the top law schools in the country: at an early gathering, the dean gave Ruth and her female classmates a hard time for taking seats away from deserving men, and that aura of sexism never really let up. Somehow, in spite of these obstacles, she managed to make *Harvard Law Review* in her second year. (*Law Review* is a prestigious, student-run journal that only the top law students are invited to join.) Her husband was a year ahead of her at Harvard and was offered a job at a top firm in New York City when he graduated, so they moved, and Ruth finished law school at Columbia—again joining *Columbia Law Review* and graduating first in her class in 1959.

In spite of her academic success, Ruth discovered that being smart—even the smartest in her class—didn't matter so much if you were also a woman. And in the world of "white shoe" law firms, being Jewish didn't help either. Being a mother was the third strike against her. The top student at a top law school, she struggled to get a job! She wound up clerking for a judge, then teaching at Rutgers Law School. There she fought for equal pay when she discovered that a male colleague had a higher salary. She also fought on behalf of female maids at Rutgers when they were laid off before male janitors and again on behalf of female employees so they would receive the same retirement benefits as men.

Wherever she went, Ruth shed a light on injustice and fought for equality. In the 1970s, she served as director and cofounder of the Women's Rights Project of the American Civil Liberties Union (ACLU), for which she argued six landmark cases on gender equality before the

US Supreme Court. She was unique in using cases of discrimination against men as a means of promoting equal rights. For example, in a 1975 case, she argued against a provision in the Social Security Act that denied widowed fathers Social Security benefits when their working wives died. She also fought on behalf of a male convict who felt that his right to a fair jury was violated because his jury did not include women, whose service was then voluntary.

Case by case, chipping away at laws she deemed unfair, Ruth helped rethink the way women were hired, compensated, and treated and, in doing so, built an impressive reputation as a crusader for equality. Women can have their own credit cards, earn equal pay, serve on juries, and much more—all thanks to RBG's work.

In 1980, she was appointed to the US Court of Appeals by President Jimmy Carter. Then in 1993, she was famously nominated for the Supreme Court by President Bill Clinton—only the second woman to serve and the first Jewish woman. At the time, membership certificates to the Supreme Court Bar were dated "in the year of Our Lord . . . 1993." Representing the concerns of other Jewish attorneys, Ruth complained to Chief Justice Roberts, who apparently agreed that "Our Lord" was not the same for everyone, and now members of the bar can have their certificates printed with simply the year.

She often talked about the deep connection between her Judaism and her life's work. In a speech she gave at the US Holocaust Memorial Museum in 2004, she said, "My heritage as a Jew and my occupation as a judge fit together symmetrically. The demand for justice runs through the entirety of Jewish history and Jewish tradition. I take pride in and draw strength from my heritage, as signs in my chambers attest: a large silver mezuzah on my door post, gift from the Shulamith School for Girls in Brooklyn; on three walls, in artists' renditions of Hebrew letters, the command from Deuteronomy: *Tzedek, tzedek, tirdof,* 'Justice, justice shall you pursue.' Those words are ever-present reminders of what judges must do that they 'may thrive.'"

During her decades on the Supreme Court, Justice Ginsburg became perhaps better known for her dissents than for her majority opinions—all read aloud and written in plain English rather than the court's usual legalese. In the case of *Burwell v. Hobby Lobby*, employers won the right to deny birth control coverage to female employees. (At that time, some insurance companies covered the cost of birth control and some did not.) In her dissent, Ruth called out her male colleagues for allowing corporations to opt out of almost any law that they find "incompatible with their sincerely held religious beliefs." She pointed out how this same premise could apply if companies had religious objections to blood transfusions, antidepressants, or anesthesia. "The court, I fear, has ventured into a minefield."

The dissent that launched the "Notorious RBG" meme came in 2013, when a 5–4 majority struck down the Voting Rights Act of 1965. While the majority argued that states no longer needed federal government oversight to insure fair elections, RBG accused them of "throwing away your umbrella in a rainstorm because you are not getting wet." She knew that the climate could easily change again— and she was right. Voting quickly became more difficult for poor Black people and Latinos. In what would become a pattern, her objections beautifully, brilliantly summarized the feelings of young progressives, earning her a loyal following.

DISSENTING WITH STYLE

Like many Jewish women, RBG had a bold sense of fashion. Whether it was her innate need for equality or style, she pointed out that justice robes were designed with men in mind, cut to show their shirt collars and ties. She felt that the female justices ought to be entitled to show a little hint of personality too. She started with a simple lace collar and over time appeared in more elaborate options. Standouts include a gold embellished jabot, given to her by her law clerks, that she wore every time she announced a majority opinion. She was also known for making a statement with a rhinestone-studded "dissent collar."

When her daughter became a law professor at Columbia, Ruth recalled how at her own law school graduation, Jane, age four, shouted from the balcony, "That's my mommy!" as Ruth accepted her diploma. Ruth Bader Ginsburg inspired not just her own daughter (and the granddaughters who call her Bubbe) but generations of women who witnessed the power of boldly speaking up for justice as RBG did so memorably over her 60-year career.

She died on the auspicious Erev Rosh Hashanah, in the fall of 2020. Millions mourned her passing with marches, vigils, and social media posts. And thousands of admirers made their way to the steps of the Supreme Court to pay tribute, and then to the Capitol where she became the first woman in history to lie in state (a rare tribute for special public servants). Jews who had spent the week reflecting on the past year found themselves looking ahead to a future that suddenly seemed dimmer.

ELENA KAGAN
1960–

When Elena Kagan was sworn in as a US Supreme Court associate justice, she became the third Jew on the court and the second Jewish woman, following Ruth Bader Ginsburg. (Justice Stephen Breyer is also Jewish.) There is nothing coincidental about a people who comprise less than 3 percent of the US population making up a third of the highest court in the land. They have all talked about the way that social justice is part of Jewish tradition. It was also an important part of Elena Kagan's childhood.

Her mother was a teacher, and Elena's father was a lawyer and community board member who represented tenants in disputes with landlords. Born in 1960, she was raised on Manhattan's liberal Upper West Side, where her family "synagogue-hopped" from Reform to Conservative to a Modern Orthodox congregation, seeking rabbis who resonated for them. They kept a kosher home, primarily so that Elena's more observant grandparents could eat there, but "we were the kind of Jews who kept a kosher home and then went out and ordered shrimp at the Chinese restaurant," she recalls.

When she was 13 and a star Hebrew school student, Elena lobbied Rabbi Shlomo Riskin at the Lincoln Square Synagogue to allow her to have a bat mitzvah. Up to that point, only boys had been called to the Torah. Rabbi Riskin recalled, "She wanted to recite a Haftorah like the boys, and she wanted her bat mitzvah on a Saturday morning."

They compromised, and instead she was allowed to read from the Book of Ruth on Friday night. Much like she would later build bridges between the conservative and liberal wings of the court, she explained, "We reached a kind of deal. It wasn't like a full bat mitzvah, but it was something." And that was a first for a girl at Lincoln Square Synagogue.

Her mother's rigor, demanding that Elena and her two brothers rewrite and revise all of their schoolwork until it was perfect, paid off as Elena went to a competitive public high school in New York City, Hunter College High School. In her high school yearbook, she is shown wearing a judge's robe and holding a gavel with a quote from Supreme Court justice Felix Frankfurter beneath her senior photo: "Government is itself an art, one of the subtlest of arts."

After graduating from Princeton University, she earned a master of philosophy degree at Cambridge University and then went on to Harvard Law School. With an impressive education behind her, Elena believed there were two ways that she could have an impact: to teach or to perform public service. She wound up doing both. After several years clerking (including a year as clerk for the first Black justice, Thurgood Marshall) and a few years in private practice, she became a law professor at the University of Chicago. She loved making an impact in this way, describing "the simple joy of teaching; of trying to communicate to students why I so love the law . . . not just because it's challenging and endlessly interesting, but because law matters."

After a stint in public service working as associate White House counsel for President Bill Clinton, she returned to academic life as a professor at Harvard Law School, where she would go on to become its first female dean.

President Obama presented her with more opportunities to make her mark through public service, appointing her as the first female solicitor general in 2009. In that role, she represented the US in cases argued before the Supreme Court. And when a seat opened up on the Supreme Court in 2010, Elena was nominated to fill it. It is standard for senators, who have to approve presidential appointments, to interview appointees before casting their votes. She has often talked about a Republican senator from Idaho who was very concerned about gun rights and asked Elena whether she had ever hunted. She explained that as a New York City kid, she hadn't had any real opportunities, but promised him that if she was approved by the Senate, she would ask Antonin Scalia (another Supreme Court justice) to take her hunting, since he was known to be a passionate hunter. When she was confirmed, Elena dutifully kept her word, explaining to Justice Scalia, "This is the only promise I made during my entire confirmation proceedings, so you have to help me fulfill it." Scalia thought that was hilarious and invited her along on the first of many hunting trips Elena would join. She cherished the new experience and her friendship with the conservative justice.

Elena's biggest claim to fame as a Jewish judge came during a case regarding separation of church and state in which a Christian town was holding prayers at the start of its town meetings. Elena and the three other liberal justices (Ruth Bader Ginsburg, Sonia Sotomayor, and Stephen Breyer) dissented from the majority opinion that this was okay. In her dissent, she invoked one of the first interactions between George Washington and American Jews.

> "I've learned that we make progress by listening to each other, across every apparent political or ideological divide."

Quoting Moses Seixas of Newport, Rhode Island, who thanked Washington in 1790 with "a deep sense of gratitude" for the new government, Kagan related Seixas's statement that the US has "a government, which to bigotry gives no sanction, to persecution no assistance—but generously affording to all liberty of conscience and immunities of citizenship: deeming every one, of whatever nation, tongue, or language, equal parts of the great governmental machine."

She included this historic quote to illustrate the significance of a government not showing preference to a specific religion. As a Jew, a legal scholar, and seeker of justice, she very well knew the importance of that concept.

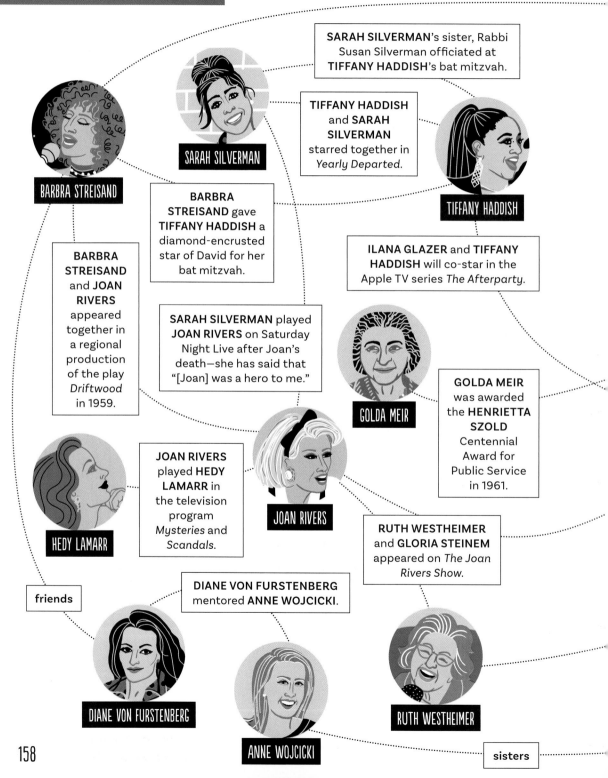

Many of the women in this book are connected to one another. It's a small Jewish world.

SARAH SILVERMAN's sister, Rabbi Susan Silverman officiated at TIFFANY HADDISH's bat mitzvah.

TIFFANY HADDISH and SARAH SILVERMAN starred together in *Yearly Departed*.

SARAH SILVERMAN

TIFFANY HADDISH

BARBRA STREISAND

BARBRA STREISAND gave TIFFANY HADDISH a diamond-encrusted star of David for her bat mitzvah.

ILANA GLAZER and TIFFANY HADDISH will co-star in the Apple TV series *The Afterparty*.

BARBRA STREISAND and JOAN RIVERS appeared together in a regional production of the play *Driftwood* in 1959.

SARAH SILVERMAN played JOAN RIVERS on Saturday Night Live after Joan's death—she has said that "[Joan] was a hero to me."

GOLDA MEIR

GOLDA MEIR was awarded the HENRIETTA SZOLD Centennial Award for Public Service in 1961.

JOAN RIVERS played HEDY LAMARR in the television program *Mysteries and Scandals*.

JOAN RIVERS

HEDY LAMARR

RUTH WESTHEIMER and GLORIA STEINEM appeared on *The Joan Rivers Show*.

DIANE VON FURSTENBERG mentored ANNE WOJCICKI.

friends

DIANE VON FURSTENBERG

ANNE WOJCICKI

RUTH WESTHEIMER

sisters

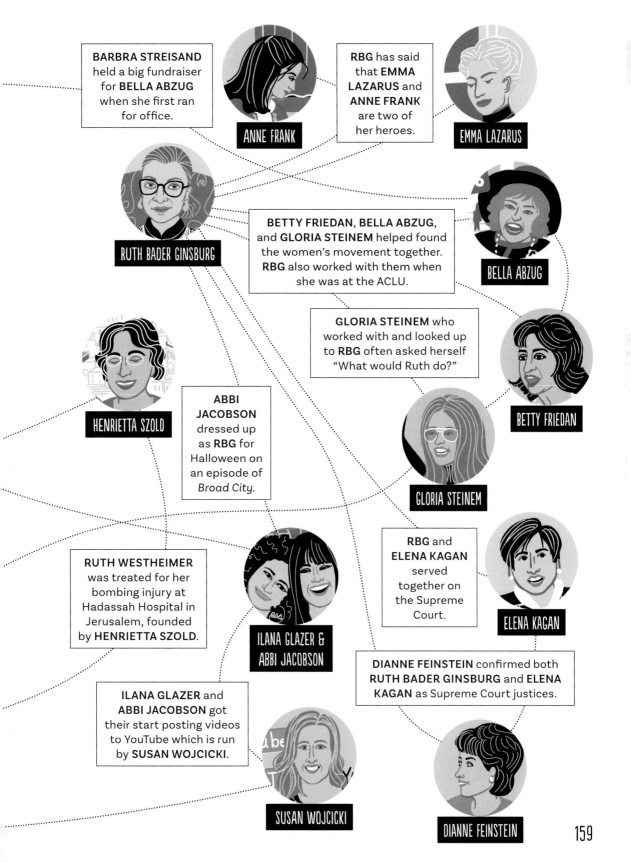

BARBRA STREISAND held a big fundraiser for **BELLA ABZUG** when she first ran for office.

ANNE FRANK

RBG has said that **EMMA LAZARUS** and **ANNE FRANK** are two of her heroes.

EMMA LAZARUS

RUTH BADER GINSBURG

BETTY FRIEDAN, BELLA ABZUG, and **GLORIA STEINEM** helped found the women's movement together. **RBG** also worked with them when she was at the ACLU.

BELLA ABZUG

GLORIA STEINEM who worked with and looked up to **RBG** often asked herself "What would Ruth do?"

HENRIETTA SZOLD

ABBI JACOBSON dressed up as **RBG** for Halloween on an episode of *Broad City*.

BETTY FRIEDAN

GLORIA STEINEM

RUTH WESTHEIMER was treated for her bombing injury at Hadassah Hospital in Jerusalem, founded by **HENRIETTA SZOLD**.

ILANA GLAZER & ABBI JACOBSON

RBG and **ELENA KAGAN** served together on the Supreme Court.

ELENA KAGAN

ILANA GLAZER and **ABBI JACOBSON** got their start posting videos to YouTube which is run by **SUSAN WOJCICKI**.

DIANNE FEINSTEIN confirmed both **RUTH BADER GINSBURG** and **ELENA KAGAN** as Supreme Court justices.

SUSAN WOJCICKI

DIANNE FEINSTEIN

RESOURCES

Check out the following books, websites, and videos if you want to learn more about some of the women in this book—or to discover more amazing Jewesses!

GENERAL READING

Jewish Virtual Library
- jewishvirtuallibrary.org
  Includes biographies as well as information about the Holocaust, religion, politics, Israel, and more

Jewish Women's Archive
- jwa.org
  Online encyclopedia that contains thousands of Jewish women's stories and historical information

Forward Association
- forward.com
  A Jewish American news media organization that covers current events

ACTIVISTS

Emma Goldman
- *Living My Life* by Emma Goldman (This is out of print but available used. It is a detailed autobiography written during the later years of her life.)

Henrietta Szold
- *To Repair A Broken World: The Life of Henrietta Szold, founder of Hadassah* by Dvora Hacohen

Betty Friedan
- *The Feminine Mystique* by Betty Friedan

Gloria Steinem
- Gloriasteinem.com
- *Gloria: In Her Own Words* (HBO documentary)
- *My Life on the Road* by Gloria Steinem
- *The Truth Will Set You Free, But First It Will Piss You off!* by Gloria Steinem

Alicia Garza
- Aliciagarza.com
- *Lady Don't Take No* (podcast)

ENTERTAINERS

Hedy Lamarr
- *Bombshell: The Hedy Lamarr Story* (PBS documentary)

Joan Rivers
- *A Piece of Work* (documentary)

Barbra Streisand
- *Funny Girl* (her first movie)
- *Yentl* (movie starring, produced, and directed by Barbra Streisand)

Sarah Silverman
- *The Bedwetter* by Sarah Silverman
- *We are Miracles* (HBO stand-up comedy special)

Tiffany Haddish
- *The Last Black Unicorn* by Tiffany Haddish

ARTISTS

Sonia Delaunay
- To view some of Sonia Delaunay's artwork, visit www.artnet.com/artists/sonia-delaunay-terk/.

Diane Arbus
- To see some of Diane Arbus's photos, visit www.artnet.com/artists/diane-arbus/.

Helen Frankenthaler
- Helen Frankenthaler's art can be seen at www.frankenthalerfoundation.org/artworks.

WRITERS

Emma Lazarus
- To read Emma Lazarus's poems, visit poetryfoundation.org and search for Emma Lazarus.

Anne Frank
- *Diary of a Young Girl* by Anne Frank

SCIENTISTS

Janet Yellen
- Janet Yellen in conversation with Paul Krugman (interview available on YouTube)

ENTREPRENEURS

Diane von Furstenberg
- *The Day Before: Diane von Furstenberg* (fashion documentary series about the days leading up to a fashion show)

LEADERS

Golda Meir
- *Lioness: Golda Meir and the Nation of Israel* by Francine Klagsbrun

JUSTICES

Ruth Bader Ginsburg
- *In My Own Words* by Ruth Bader Ginsburg
- *RBG: Hero. Icon. Dissenter.* (documentary)

OUTRAGEOUS HILARIOUS NO-HOLDS-BARRED UNAPOLOGETIC GIFTED EXTRA
OLD RENOWNED AMBITIOUS GLAMOROUS EMPOWERING VISIONARY DEVOTED
EN RADICAL GROUNDBREAKING POWERFUL GAME-CHANGING INVENTIVE RE
Y FASCINATING SUBVERSIVE COLORFUL CONTROVERSIAL PROLIFIC ENLIGHT
ARING FEARLESS UNBREAKABLE TRAILBLAZING COURAGEOUS TIRELESS NOT
LIENT ICONIC OUTRAGEOUS HILARIOUS NO-HOLDS-BARRED UNAPOLOGETIC
NG PASSIONATE BOLD RENOWNED AMBITIOUS GLAMOROUS EMPOWERING VI
OUS BRILLIANT DRIVEN RADICAL GROUNDBREAKING POWERFUL GAME-CHAN
GIFTED EXTRAORDINARY FASCINATING SUBVERSIVE COLORFUL CONTROVER
VISIONARY DEVOTED DARING FEARLESS UNBREAKABLE TRAILBLAZING COU
NGING INVENTIVE RESILIENT ICONIC OUTRAGEOUS HILARIOUS NO-HOLDS-B
AL PROLIFIC ENLIGHTENING PASSIONATE BOLD RENOWNED AMBITIOUS GLAM
RAGEOUS TIRELESS NOTORIOUS BRILLIANT DRIVEN RADICAL GROUNDBREAKI
OLDS-BARRED UNAPOLOGETIC GIFTED EXTRAORDINARY FASCINATING SUBVE
S GLAMOROUS EMPOWERING VISIONARY DEVOTED DARING FEARLESS UNBRE
EAKING POWERFUL GAME-CHANGING INVENTIVE RESILIENT ICONIC OUTRAG
VERSIVE COLORFUL CONTROVERSIAL PROLIFIC ENLIGHTENING PASSIONATE
NBREAKABLE TRAILBLAZING COURAGEOUS TIRELESS NOTORIOUS BRILLIANT
RAGEOUS HILARIOUS NO-HOLDS-BARRED UNAPOLOGETIC GIFTED EXTRAORD
OLD RENOWNED AMBITIOUS GLAMOROUS EMPOWERING VISIONARY DEVOTE
EN RADICAL GROUNDBREAKING POWERFUL GAME-CHANGING INVENTIVE RE
Y FASCINATING SUBVERSIVE COLORFUL CONTROVERSIAL PROLIFIC ENLIGHT
ARING FEARLESS UNBREAKABLE TRAILBLAZING COURAGEOUS TIRELESS NO
LIENT ICONIC OUTRAGEOUS HILARIOUS NO-HOLDS-BARRED UNAPOLOGETIC

AL GROUNDBREAKING POWERFUL GAME-CHANGING INVENTIVE RESILIENT IC
SUBVERSIVE COLORFUL CONTROVERSIAL PROLIFIC ENLIGHTENING PASSIONA
UNBREAKABLE TRAILBLAZING COURAGEOUS TIRELESS NOTORIOUS BRILLIANT
TRAGEOUS HILARIOUS NO-HOLDS-BARRED UNAPOLOGETIC GIFTED EXTRAORD
E BOLD RENOWNED AMBITIOUS GLAMOROUS EMPOWERING VISIONARY DEVOT
DRIVEN RADICAL GROUNDBREAKING POWERFUL GAME-CHANGING INVENTIVE
ARY FASCINATING SUBVERSIVE COLORFUL CONTROVERSIAL PROLIFIC ENLIGH
DARING FEARLESS UNBREAKABLE TRAILBLAZING COURAGEOUS TIRELESS N
VE RESILIENT ICONIC OUTRAGEOUS HILARIOUS NO-HOLDS-BARRED UNAPOLOG
LIGHTENING PASSIONATE BOLD RENOWNED AMBITIOUS GLAMOROUS EMPOWE
NOTORIOUS BRILLIANT DRIVEN RADICAL GROUNDBREAKING POWERFUL GAME
ETIC GIFTED EXTRAORDINARY FASCINATING SUBVERSIVE COLORFUL CONTROV
WERING VISIONARY DEVOTED DARING FEARLESS UNBREAKABLE TRAILBLAZING
UL GAME-CHANGING INVENTIVE RESILIENT ICONIC OUTRAGEOUS HILARIOUS N
ONTROVERSIAL PROLIFIC ENLIGHTENING PASSIONATE BOLD RENOWNED AMB
AZING COURAGEOUS TIRELESS NOTORIOUS BRILLIANT DRIVEN RADICAL GROUN
US NO-HOLDS-BARRED UNAPOLOGETIC GIFTED EXTRAORDINARY FASCINATING
AMBITIOUS GLAMOROUS EMPOWERING VISIONARY DEVOTED DARING FEARLE
GROUNDBREAKING POWERFUL GAME-CHANGING INVENTIVE RESILIENT ICONIC
SUBVERSIVE COLORFUL CONTROVERSIAL PROLIFIC ENLIGHTENING PASSIONA
UNBREAKABLE TRAILBLAZING COURAGEOUS TIRELESS NOTORIOUS BRILLIANT
UTRAGEOUS HILARIOUS NO-HOLDS-BARRED UNAPOLOGETIC GIFTED EXTRAORD
E BOLD RENOWNED AMBITIOUS GLAMOROUS EMPOWERING VISIONARY DEVOT
DRIVEN RADICAL GROUNDBREAKING POWERFUL GAME-CHANGING INVENTIV